Retirement Plan

MW01699625

Planning for *Early Retirement*

Larry J. Stubbs
B.Sc., CFP, RFP, CIM

CCH Now You Know®

CCH CANADIAN LIMITED
90 Sheppard Avenue East, Suite 300,
North York, ON M2N 6X1
Telephone: (416) 224-2248 Toll Free: 1-800-461-5308
Fax: (416) 224-2243 Toll Free: 1-800-461-4131
Internet: http://www.ca.cch.com

Published by CCH Canadian Limited

Canadian Cataloguing in Publication Data

Stubbs, Larry, 1954-
Planning for early retirement: key concepts for financial freedom

(Financial advisors series)
Includes index.
ISBN 1055141-353-1

1. Finance, Personal. 2. Retirement income — Canada — Planning. 3. Early retirement — Canada — Planning. I. Title. II. Series.

HG179.S775 1999 332.024'01 C99-932844-1

Typeset and printed in Canada by CCH Canadian Limited.

OVERVIEW

All financial planning including retirement decision-making should be based upon the following six-step process:

1. Identify and clarify the current situation

This first step involves data gathering and a review of quantitative information such as the investors total assets and liabilities which comprise the net worth statement, cash flow statement, insurance policies, tax returns, wills, powers of attorney, investment portfolio and transactions, employee benefit booklets, trust agreements, pension statements, and some basic family history such as name, age, marital status, employment history, details of the children's birth dates and other qualitative details. Essentially this step summarizes where the client is today. An individual's current situation is a result of the cumulative effects of all of the financial decisions and transactions that have occurred in the past up until the current time.

2. Identify goals and objectives

This activity seeks to identify both financial and personal goals and objectives. After identification and listing, the goals and objectives need to be prioritized, to facilitate the allocation of the available resources to the most critical concerns.

It is of primary importance that the financial goals are measurable, in order to track success and to provide feedback so that strategies can be fine-tuned. Goals must be:

Specific

Otherwise, they are not goals, they are merely dreams. "I require $500,000 by my 65th birthday" is an example of a specific goal. "I want to be rich when I retire" is a dream, not a goal.

Measurable

Financial goals are easily measurable since dollars and cents can be counted.

Attainable

Goals must be securable.

Realistic

In order for a goal to be achieved, it must be within the realm of reason. To accumulate $1 million by age 65, if one is currently age 64, and has no savings may be attainable by winning a lottery however; this is unrealistic. Conversely, for a 25-year-old to accumulate $1 million by age 65 through saving and investing is probably both attainable and realistic.

Time bound

All goals should be time bound in order to track progress towards the goal's completion and to provide feedback. Corrections should be made in the action plan therefore maximizing the probability of success.

Bringing it back on track

If goals are determined to be unattainable and/or unrealistic, the individual can do one or more of the following to get back on track:

- reduce discretionary expenditures,
- increase income,
- choose more aggressive investments, with potentially higher investment returns,
- increase the timeframe over which to obtain the goal, or
- reduce the dollar value of the goal.

3. Analyze problems and opportunities

An analysis of the current situation will allow for the identification of additional opportunities that can be exploited in order to more efficiently accomplish the specified financial goals. Moreover, the situational analysis will help to identify problems that may be acting as obstacles or preventing the most efficient accomplishment of the identified objectives. Problems must be identified before solutions can be established.

It is in this stage of the financial planning process that the use of various mathematical tools is most powerful.

The answers to questions like "Should I pay off my mortgage or contribute to my RRSP this year?" are not straightforward. The answer will depend upon each individual's situation, and the assumptions that the individual makes such as the interest rate, the rate of inflation, and the chosen investment vehicles. It is imperative that the economic assumptions upon which the financial plan will be based be set by the individual (with input from the financial advisor). It is therefore necessary that some basic understanding of the interrelationship of key economic information and investment performance be acquired in order to make educated or enlightened financial decisions.

4. Develop solutions

If sufficient analysis has been performed in the previous step of the process, the development of solutions is straightforward.

5. Implementation

This step involves putting the financial plan into action. An implementation and action plan should be created with appropriate strategies and tactics outlined in writing.

6. Monitor and review

The final step in the financial planning process is the ongoing monitoring that is required in order to fine-tune the financial plan and to ensure the successful attainment of the specified financial objectives. Regular reviews and updates allow any plan, which has gone off track to be quickly, set back onto the rails.

Regular review allows for any changes in an individual's lifestyle or in the economic environment to be reassessed. Additionally, a review allows the opportunity to provide for any changes to strategies or tactics, which might be required.

The critical disciplines

There are six fundamental subject areas or critical disciplines which must be inter-woven into any plan for early retirement. The critical disciplines are the basic areas of knowledge upon which the financial plan must be based. These foundations are the essence of the plan. Each subject area overlaps another and weaves itself throughout the financial planning process.

Tax planning

Tax planning is important and is integrated throughout all of the disciplines. Tax will have a major impact upon an individual's goals and the accomplishment of those goals.

Cash and credit/debt management

Most individuals must use credit to build their net worth. This creates cash management concerns.

Retirement planning

It is never too early to commence retirement planning. In fact, the earlier one starts, the easier it is to attain one's goals in the end.

Investment planning

A major part of building net worth or creating retirement funds involves investment.

Insurance and risk management

The majority of individuals insure their homes and vehicles. Insuring one's life and protecting the continuity of the individual's income stream is critical.

Estate planning

Estate planning includes providing for heirs and protecting loved ones through prudent estate pre-planning.

PREFACE

All of the six critical disciplines referred to in the preceding Overview are key to planning for early retirement. In order to understand how each discipline relates to an individual's situation, the planner must be able to grasp the determining factors, rules and strategies. In this book, the reader will be introduced to many ideas and concepts that can be used to build a successful early retirement plan. Several diagnostic tools will be presented, allowing the reader to evaluate existing retirement plans and make any necessary adjustments.

In addition to the key concepts, many of the chapters also contain a glossary as well as checklists, questions and answers, and appendicies. Broad in its scope, this work is not meant to be totally comprehensive in all subject areas. Entire textbooks are dedicated to the topics of estate planning, financial statement analysis, and the valuation of stocks and bonds. The intent is to provide the reader with insights into some basic tools and processes in order that they may develop and sharpen their analytical skills to facilitate the efficient achievement of the ultimate goal, which is early retirement.

TABLE OF CONTENTS

CHAPTER 1

Financial Decision Making

The goal of financial planning is to increase and maximize investable net worth through the effective manipulation of money and credit.

An investor's ability to maximize investable net worth is greatly aided by the ability to choose amongst competing investment options. Various formulae and tools can be used by investors to determine the extant value or the past performance of their investments.

Analytical tools

Depending on the type of investment that is owned or under consideration by an investor, various tools may be used to measure and evaluate the return or value of that investment.

Much of financial planning requires answers to mathematical questions that involve the time value of money. The time value of money (TVM) represents the trade-off between the present use and the future gain of money. Time value of money moves all money flows either back to the present or out to a common future date. It measures the costs and benefits of investment alternatives that occur in different time periods. The most common example is when an investor gives money to someone else, who subsequently puts it to work, and then pays the investor interest in return for the use of the investor's money. This interest is compensation for the temporary loss to the investor of the use of the money invested.

Although it is possible to compute all time value of money problems mathematically using formulae or by the use of compound interest tables, computers and financial calculators add simplicity and efficiency to these computations.

Compound interest is interest earned on both principal and interest. Interest is compounded when it is computed, added to the principal amount, and reinvested. The process of calculating the future sum or value (FV) of an investment is called compounding.

The process of calculating the present value (PV) of a future sum is called discounting.

Compounding and discounting are reciprocals of one another. This means they are inverse mathematical functions of one another.

An annuity is defined as a series of payments or receipts of a fixed dollar amount, for a specified number of time periods.

An ordinary annuity assumes that these payments or receipts occur at the end of the period. Conversely, an annuity due assumes that the payments or receipts occur at the beginning of the period. In finance, the usual assumption, or norm, is the use of an ordinary annuity i.e. payments or receipts occurring at the end of the period. The use of an annuity due is signaled via key words such as … "starting today", "immediately", "starting now" or words to a similar effect.

A perpetuity is a special type of an annuity that has no maturity date. An example of a perpetuity is a preferred share that pays a fixed and stated dividend amount forever.

Capital budgeting is different from cash flow budgeting and provides additional analytical benefits to an investor. Capital budgeting is the process, commonly employed in corporate finance, of allocating capital to investments whose benefits will be spread over several time periods. Typically, an investor is faced with more potential investment choices than can be successfully undertaken because of the lack of funds. Capital rationing therefore must occur when there is an upper limit or maximum amount placed on the ability to invest or with which to make capital expenditures. The investor requires some sound and logical methods by which to rank potential investments in order to make reasonable capital rationing decisions.

Capital budgeting evaluates an investment's incremental cash flows and evaluates these cash flows relative to an investment's cost. Capital budgeting uses cash flows rather than profits because the cash flows better reflect the timing of both the costs and benefits of an investment decision. Specifically, only the incremental after-tax cash flows are used when determining whether to undertake a particular investment.

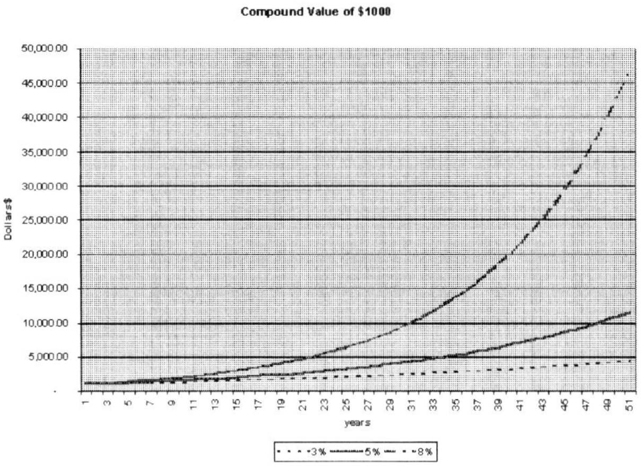

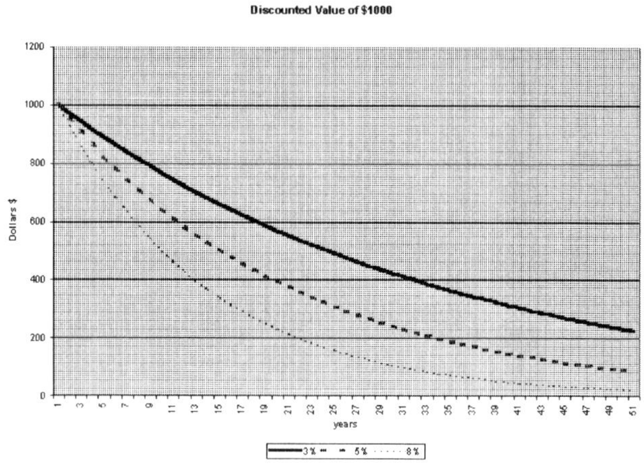

Net present value (NPV) is a method used in evaluating and ranking investments, whereby the net present value of all cash outflows (such as the cost of the investment) and cash inflows (such as the investment's return) are calculated using a given discount or hurdle rate. An investment is considered acceptable if the NPV is positive. NPV is used to rank different investment options, from the highest NPV to the lowest NPV. An investment is rejected if the NPV is negative since this indicates that the investment does not improve the investor's current net worth.

Internal rate of return (IRR) is the discount or hurdle rate at which the present value (PV) of all of the future cash flows of an investment exactly equal the total cost of the investment. The IRR is a special case of the net present value calculation because the IRR is the rate of return at which the NPV of an investment equals zero. An investor should compute both the NPV and the IRR for each potential investment in order to verify, or provide additional insights into, the merits of a particular investment choice. Without the use of a computer or financial calculator the calculation of the IRR is done by a process known as iteration, which can be extremely time-consuming and frustrating.

IRR ranks various investments differently than NPV, if:

(1) 2 projects have different initial investments, and when

(2) the timing of the cash flows from the investments is different.

Capitalization (Cap) rate can be referred to as the capitalization rate of an asset. The Cap rate is the interest rate used to convert a series of future payments into a single present value (PV) and is commonly used in valuing real estate.

Payback period is the length of time required to recover an initial investment. The payback period is calculated as the original investment divided by annual cash flow. It can also be referred to as a cash recovery period.

The dividend discount model (DDM) is a valuation technique used for estimating the intrinsic value of a stock. DDM models calculate the discounted present value of all future dividends or future earnings. DDMs describe the relationship between a stock's current price and the present value of all future dividend payments or earnings. The most commonly used DDM assumes that, for a mature firm, the dividend stream will grow indefinitely at a constant rate. This constant growth model can be used to determine the value of a common stock.

The Gordon growth model (also known as the constant growth DDM)

$$\text{Value of a common stock} = P_0 = \frac{D_1}{(k_s - g)} = \frac{D_0(1 + g)}{(k_s - g)}$$

where

P_0 = current market stock price
D_0 = current dividend just paid
D_1 = dividend paid 1 year from now
k_s = required rate of return on a stock investment
g = long term sustainable growth rate of the stock

Return on equity (ROE) is the after-tax profit earned by a company compared to the total cost of its equity shares.

Return on assets (ROA) is the after-tax profit compared to the firms total tangible assets.

Return on investment (ROI) or return on invested capital can be defined as the after-tax profit earned by a corporation compared to the firms total invested capital. Total invested capital includes common and preferred equity plus all funded debt.

Keeping score: types of returns

Investment returns are the rewards for investing. Return includes both realized current income (interest, dividends, rent, realized capital gains or losses) and any unrealized capital appreciation or depreciation.

Types of return include:

- **Nominal return.** The named or stated rate of return.
- **Real return.** Adjusts the nominal return for the effect of inflation, and it is estimated as the nominal rate of return minus the rate of inflation equals real rate of return. A more exact formula calculates the real return as: (1+ nominal) divided by (1+ rate of inflation).
- **Effective annual rate (EAR).** The effective annual rate adjusts the nominal interest rate for the effects of compounding, when interest is compounded more often than annually.
- **Risk-free return** is the return on a risk-free asset that is earned with perfect certainty. This hypothetical return is usually proxied by federal government securities that have the same term to maturity as the investor's time horizon. For example, an investor with a 5-year time horizon would choose a 5-year government of Canada bond as the risk-free benchmark.
- **After-tax real rate of return.** Adjusts the nominal rate of return for the effects of inflation and income taxes and it is estimated as the nominal return less income taxes and the effects of inflation.
- **Holding period return (HPR).** The difference in value of an asset (current income plus or minus capital change) that occurs from the time that the asset is acquired until some future time, usually when the asset is disposed of.
- **Realized vs. non-realized gains/losses.** A realized gain on an asset is one that is actually taken and the investor has cash in hand. An example of a realized gain is when a rental property purchased for $200,000 is sold for $250,000, thus realizing a $50,000 gain. An unrealized gain on the other hand, is merely a paper profit and might be lost if the asset's value declines. No funds are exchanged and no sale is completed in the case of an unrealized gain.

What is value?

Value has a number of meanings and will be defined and used differently by various financial advisors. Value can be stated as the book value. Book value is an accounting term, which employs historic cost as opposed to the current cost of an asset. Book value is typically the value shown on the balance sheet of a company.

Current fair market value (FMV) is the observed value of an asset as it trades in the marketplace; or FMV can be defined as the appraised value.

Liquidation value is the value that an asset would bring if it were to be sold.

Intrinsic value is the value obtained from a valuation model and is compared to the current fair market price (FMV).

Although there are many types of value definitions, in general, the value of an asset is determined by three factors:

(1) The amount and timing of expected future cash inflows,

(2) The riskiness of these future cash flows, and

(3) The investor's required rate of return.

Glossary

Annual percentage rate (APR). An annualized interest rate that ignores the effects of compounding. It is calculated by multiplying the periodic interest rate by the number of periods in a year. Bond yields are typically calculated by this method.

Book value per common share. Assuming no preferred shares outstanding, the book value per common share is calculated as the total assets minus total liabilities divided by the average number of common shares outstanding.

Capital cost allowance (CCA). The amount an owner of an income producing asset is allowed to deduct for income tax purposes as a result of owning a depreciable asset. CCA is a tax shield that allows an investor to deduct the cost of depreciating capital assets from income. Under the *Income Tax Act*, Revenue Canada regards this as a necessary expense for producing income. Investors calculate CCA so that it allows a recovery over time, of the original amount invested. Generally, investors may claim only 50% of the allowable CCA expense in the year of acquisition.

Capitalization or capital structure. Total dollar amounts of all permanent sources of financing. Calculated as the total of all negotiated debt, preferred and common stock, contributed surplus and retained earnings of the company.

Capitalization method. A method of appraising real estate. Calculated as net operating income (NOI) divided by the property's current fair market value (FMV).

Cash flow. One measure of a company's financial status. Cash flow can be calculated directly or indirectly. One technique of reconstructing a cash flow statement calculates cash flow as net income for a period plus any non-cash deductions, such as depreciation, amortization, depletion, deferred income taxes, and minority interest.

Depreciation. Depreciation is an accounting expense that allows for the deduction of the initial cost of an asset over subsequent periods. The amount by which the value of improvements has decreased over time, because of wear and tear. The periodic costs of owning depreciable assets (such as buildings and equipment) that are subject to deterioration. No depreciation expense can be taken on land.

Dilution. The reduction of earnings per common share assuming all convertible securities are converted to common shares.

Fair market value (FMV). The current market price at which an asset passes from a willing seller to an interested buyer.

Fixed asset. A balance sheet item. Tangible, long-term assets that are held for use by the business and used to earn revenue. Examples are real estate or equipment.

Effective annual interest rate (EAR). The interest rate as if it were compounded only once per year. The periodic interest rate times the number of compound periods in the year equals the effective annual rate (EAR). The EAR is the actual interest rate earned/paid after adjusting the nominal or stated interest rate for the frequency of compounding employed.

Effective interest rate. The periodic interest rate considering both the frequency of compounding and the nominal rate of interest.

Equity or Shareholders' Equity or Stockholders Equity. The residual ownership interest of common and preferred shareholders. It is calculated using total assets minus total liabilities of a company. Also referred to as net worth.

Income method or investment method. An appraisal method typically used for valuing rental real estate. This valuation tool converts the net income stream produced by the property into a market value by using a capitalization rate.

Inflation risk. is the likelihood that the real return of the fixed-income investment will be less than the nominal (dollar) return. Inflation risk is referred to as the risk of unanticipated increases in future inflation.

Intangible asset. An asset with no physical form, e.g., goodwill.

Intrinsic value. The real and true value of a security. This value can be different from the market price, and it can be different from the accounting book value.

Iteration. A mathematical process in which a series of operations is repeated until an answer is derived. It is a method of approximating and deriving an answer by repeatedly re-computing until a solution is arrived at.

Leverage. The use of debt to finance the purchase and ownership of investments. The use of debt magnifies the potential variations of yields on the equity portion of the investment.

Net operating income (NOI). Gross revenue minus vacancy allowance, bad debt allowance, and total operating expenses. NOI is calculated excluding income tax, mortgage payments, and depreciation expense.

Opportunity cost. The earnings potential of an investment that is passed up in favor of current consumption or by choosing an alternate investment.

Physical depreciation. The loss in value of a depreciable asset due to wear and tear.

Preferred stock. The nonvoting class of share capital that is entitled to a dividend payment before the company pays dividends to the common shareholders. Preferred stock also has preference over the common shareholders with respect to claims on the company's assets in the case of liquidation.

Straight-line depreciation method. One of the allowable methods used to calculate depreciation expense for accounting purposes. The annual depreciation expense is calculated as purchase price minus expected salvage value divided by the economic lifetime.

Real interest rate. The nominal rate of interest minus the inflation rate, where the inflation rate is defined as the percentage change in the Consumer Price Index (CPI).

Rule of 72. Approximates a compound growth rate an investor would require in order to double the original investment. 72 divided by the interest rate equals the time required for this doubling of capital to occur.

Treasury shares. Common stocks that the company has repurchased in the marketplace are called treasury stock. In addition, treasury shares consist of those shares that are authorized for sale by the company but that are not yet issued.

Valuation. The determination or calculation of the worth, at a specified date or time, of an asset or investment.

Questions

1) How can a capitalization rate (Cap rate) be used by an investor?

The capitalization rate (Cap rate) is typically used when evaluating and analyzing real estate investments. The Cap rate is calculated by dividing net operating income (NOI) by the property's current fair market value (FMV). Alternatively, this formula can also be rearranged algebraically, and can be used to calculate the maximum amount that an investor would be prepared to pay for a piece of real estate, when the Cap rate is known.

2) Why should an investor use mathematical tools when investing?

Many individuals are frightened by the thought of having to perform mathematical calculations no doubt dredging up distasteful memories of high school algebra classes. However, with the use of technology in the form of hand-held calculators and computer programs, this anxiety and stress is unnecessary. We have included several Websites in this book that we have found particularly useful in aiding students and investors to overcome the dread of mathematics.

Mathematical tools are important to an investor in several respects. The use of mathematics is necessary and helpful when an investor is setting goals and determining the realism of these objectives. Mathematics is used to determine the amount that is required to be saved on a regular basis in order for an investor to achieve the type of retirement desired. Knowledge of mathematics also allows the investor to formulate "what if" scenarios. For example, the investor may wish to know how long their retirement nest egg will last, given a certain level of consumption in retirement, or the interest rate that is required to achieve their retirement objectives. The investor may wish to investigate the effects of different interest rates on their required savings or on their level of consumption during retirement. Employing modern portfolio theory, since risk and reward are related, it stands to reason that if an investor requires an interest rate of 20%, to reach their retirement goals, then an investor will obviously have to consider their risk tolerance in their choice of investment compared with an individual who requires a 5% return in order to achieve the same level of consumption during retirement.

Many companies provide investors with excellent mathematical tools. However, the investor must bear in mind that these companies are not altruistic and that they have other motives, which may not be precisely identical to the objectives of the investor. If the investor is unaware of the method used in a computation, then the investor must rely on the assumptions and methods of the other party. Basic mathematics skills allow the investor to make their own decisions and use their own assumptions in order to arrive at individual answers to their own questions. No one has a greater stake in an individual's retirement plan than the individual himself or herself. In other words, the best defense is a good offense!

3) A term deposit pays 5% interest. What is the nominal rate?

The nominal rate is a named or stated rate. In this case, the nominal rate is 5%.

4) If a customer it is charged 2.75% interest rate, compounded monthly, on a department store credit card, how much is the annual interest rate?

An individual who does not understand the time value of money would simply calculate that the annual interest rate is $12 \times (0.0275)$ which equals 33%. This is known as the annual percentage rate (APR), and although it is commonly used, it does not take compounding into account. In order to calculate the annual interest rate that is actually charged the investor must use the effective annual rate (EAR), which accounts for both the frequency of compounding and the nominal rate. The effective annual rate is calculated as:

$EAR = (1 + .0275)^{12} - 1 = (1.0275)^{12} - 1 = 38.48\%$ annually, a significant difference!

The following questions can be answered using a financial calculator,

where the necessary keystrokes on the calculator are as follows:
n = number of compounding periods
i = interest rate per compounding period
pmt = periodic payment
PV = present value
FV = future value
NPV = net present value
CFo, CFi,CF2,CF3 = cash flow function keys
IRR = internal rate of return

5) An investor is putting $2,000 per year into a mutual fund that averages a return of 9% per year. How many years will these payments

have to be made before the fund will be worth $100,000 (rounded to the nearest whole number of years)

i = 9%, pmt = ($2,000), FV = $100,000 Compute n.

n = 20 years (rounded up to the nearest whole number)

6) The common stock of XYZ Inc. is currently selling in the market for $36.67. XYZ Inc. has just paid its annual dividend $2.00, and the dividend is expected to grow at 10% per year indefinitely. What rate of return can an investor expect to earn on this investment in XYZ Inc. stock?

This question can be answered by algebraically manipulating the formula for the constant growth dividend discount model, and solving for k.

$$P_0 = \frac{D_1}{(k_s - g)}$$

$$k_s = \frac{D_1}{P_0} + g = \frac{D_0(1 + g)}{P_0} + g = \frac{\$2.00(1.10)}{\$36.67} + 0.10 = \frac{\$2.20}{\$36.67} + 0.10 = .15999$$

Therefore, an investor in the stock of XYZ Inc. can expect to earn a 16% rate of return.

7) An insurance salesperson offers an annuity contract that will pay $100,000 after 20 years if the annuitant pays $2,000 per year with the first payment due immediately. What rate of return is being offered?

Note: this question requires the use of an annuity due in the calculation! Be sure to switch the calculator to Begin mode.

n = 20 years, pmt = ($2,000) per year, FV = $100,000, Compute i.

i = 8.10%

8) Find the Net Present Value (NPV) of the following cash flow schedule using a 10% discount rate:

Year	Cash Flow
0	$(3,000)
1	(5,000)
2	2,000
3	4,000
4	6,000
5	(1,000)

This question uses the net present value function of the financial calculator.

CFo = ($3,000), CFi = ($5,000), CF2 = $2,000, CF3 = $4,000, CF4 = $6,000, CF5 = ($1,000),

i = 10%, Compute NPV.

NPV = $589.86

9) Calculate the internal rate of return (IRR) of a $10,000 investment that is expected to produce the following cash flows:

Year	Cash Flow
2	$ 7,000
3	6,000
4	3,000

This question uses the internal rate of return (IRR) functions of the financial calculator.

CFo = ($10,000), CFi = $0, CF2 = $7,000, CF3 = $6,000, CF4 = $3,000, Compute IRR.

IRR = 19.00%

NOTE! Be sure that the first cash flow (CFi) is entered as $0.

10) The earnings of the ABC Company are currently $2.00 per share. If the earnings per share grow over the next 5 years at an annual growth rate of 10%, how much will they be at the end of that time?

n = 5 years, i = 10%, PV = $2.00, Compute FV.

FV = $3.22

11) A stock is expected to pay an annual dividend of $0, $2, and $4 per share at the end of each of the next three years, respectively. At the end of the third year, the stock is expected to sell for $80 per share. If the stock is currently selling at $50 per share, what is the expected return on a three-year investment in this stock?

This question can be solved using the internal rate of return functions of the financial calculator.

CFo = ($50), CFi = $0, CF2 = $2, CF3 = $4 + $80 = $84, Compute IRR.

IRR = 20.00%

NOTE. The third cash flow includes the $4 dividend plus the $80 sale price of the stock. The first cash flow of zero dollars at the end of the first-year must be entered into the calculator.

Appendix

The Mathematics of Finance

Essential Symbols

FV = future value

PV = present value

k = nominal interest rate

n = number years

pmt = periodic payment

m = number of compounding periods in year

i = periodic interest rate; interest rate per compound period

infl = annual rate of inflation

k_{real} = real interest rate

EAR = effective annual interest rate

NPV = net present value

IRR = internal rate of return

CF_0 = initial cash flow

CF_t = cash flow in period

P_0 = current market price

D_0 = current cash dividends just paid

D_t = dividend expected in year

I_t = interest earned in year

M = par or maturity value of a bond

MTR = marginal tax rate

s = sample standard deviation

Future Value of $1

$FV = PV\ (1 + k)^n$

Present Value of $1

$$PV = \frac{FV_n}{(1 + k)^n}$$

Net Present Value (NPV)

$$NPV = \sum_{t=1}^{n} \frac{CF_t}{(1 + k)^n} - CF_0$$

Internal Rate of Return (IRR)

$$\sum_{t=1}^{n} \frac{CF_t}{(1 + IRR)^t} - CF_0 = 0$$

Present Value of a Perpetuity

$$P_0 = \frac{PMT}{k}$$

Present Value of an Annuity of $1

$$PV = PMT \times \left[\frac{1 - \frac{1}{(1 + k)^n}}{k} \right]$$

Future Value of an Annuity of $1

$$FV = PMT \times \left[\frac{(1 + k)^n - 1}{k} \right]$$

Future Value of $1 with more Frequent than annual Compounding

$$FV_n = PV\,[1 + (k/m)]^{nm}$$

Present Value of an Annuity Due of $1

$$PV = PMT \times \left[\frac{1 - \frac{1}{(1 + k)^n}}{k} \right](1 + k)$$

Future Value of an Annuity Due of $1

$$FV = PMT \times \left[\frac{(1 + k)^n - 1}{k} \right](1 + k)$$

Effective Annual Compound Interest Rate

$$EAR = \left[1 + \frac{k_{nominal}}{m}\right]^{m} - 1$$

Annual Percentage Rate

$$APR = m \times i$$

Real Rate of Return

$$(1 + k_{real}) = \frac{(1 + k_{nominal})}{(1 + infl)}$$

Capitalization rate or Cap rate

$$CapRate = \frac{\text{Net Operating Income}}{\text{Current Market Value}} = \frac{NOI}{FMV}$$

CHAPTER 2

Credit, Debt and Cash Management

Credit, Debt and Cash Management

Most Canadians will incur some form of indebtedness, whether it is in the form of a mortgage, vehicle loan, or credit card debt, at some point during their working lives. Ensuring that debt, and its inherent cost, is minimized before retirement will provide a retiree with a more positive cash flow.

Credit can be defined as a financial transaction that involves the lending of money and the transfer of property with the promise of repayment by a fixed maturity date. The transfer of property in a credit transaction is only intended to be a temporary expedient.

The lender is the grantor of credit, and is known as the creditor. The borrower is said to be the debtor. Credit and debt, and the lender and the borrower are therefore, on opposite sides of the same coin.

Debt is a contractual obligation that is enforceable by law.

The cost of debt is a function of the principal borrowed, the interest rate charged, and the frequency with which the interest is compounded. The interest rate charged by the creditor is the price of the loan and the rate reflects the creditor's risk. Generally speaking, the more frequently that interest is compounded the worse it is for the debtor in terms of total interest costs. Conversely, the more often that interest is compounded, the better the situation from the creditor's perspective.

A consumer can arrange credit so that it is open-ended, closed-ended, secured, or unsecured. Revolving credit is also known as open-ended credit. Under the terms of a revolving credit arrangement a limit is pre-authorized and extended. The consumer determines when and the amount of credit to be drawn, and is only required to pay a minimum amount, usually monthly. In other words, this credit line can be charged up and paid down within the pre-authorized restrictions. Common examples of revolving credit would include credit cards and lines of credit.

Credit also exists in a closed-end form. According to this arrangement, the debtor must pay the principal plus interest according to a pre-arranged and agreed-upon schedule. An example of this type of credit is a mortgage.

Finally, credit can be arranged as either secured or unsecured. Security is usually provided either in the form of collateral or by a specific guarantee. Generally speaking, all else being equal, a secured loan carries less risk than an unsecured loan and therefore a secured loan carries a lower interest rate.

The advantages of using credit

- Having pre-arranged credit minimizes the need to carry cash or a checkbook. As long as re-payments are made promptly, having credit is a convenience.
- A consumer can more easily make large purchases immediately rather than having to wait and save enough cash to pay for the purchase. This can sometimes be viewed as a form of forced savings.
- Conveniently able to make purchases using telephone, fax, or over the Internet.
- Can be viewed as a source of funding in case of emergency.
- The ability to buy now rather than having to wait can be advantageous in an inflationary economic environment. Borrowers tend to benefit more than creditors during periods of inflation.
- Financing the purchase of investment assets with debt generally increases net worth over time, and can be structured in order to minimize the income tax consequences, which then effectively becomes a tax shelter.

The disadvantages of credit

- The convenience of having credit available means living with the temptation of impulse buying.
- Problems can arise if one loses track of spending between statement dates.
- Underestimating the true cost of credit. The interest cost on unpaid balances can be very high, especially for credit cards. Some of the information provided by the grantors of credit is not easily understood. In addition to interest cost, a borrower must also consider any additional hidden fees, which increase the cost of borrowing. Additional cost may be incurred for life insurance, disability insurance, and other loan enhancements.
- There is a potential security risk of giving credit details over the telephone, fax, or Internet to unauthorized parties.
- The loss of financial flexibility and freedom due to the increase in ongoing fixed interest cost, and the commitment of future income to debt repayment.

- The magnification of losses when using leveraged investments, which perform poorly.
- Borrowing to finance the purchase of depreciable property or for current consumption can decrease net worth.

The C's of Credit

These factors are considered by all lenders, in varying degrees, when they review requests for credit.

Character

Character refers to the borrower's reputation. Researching a borrower's reputation will involve looking at past payment performance and a review of spending habits to date. One important question from the lenders perspective is the purpose of the loan. The lender is concerned with the quality of the loan's purpose; an acceptable purpose for a loan is to borrow funds to buy a home. It might be considered a poor purpose to try to obtain a loan to pay out a bankruptcy debt.

Capacity

Here the lender is considering the debtor's ability to re-pay the loan and interest in a timely manner. The lender will be interested in reviewing the borrowers continuity of income. Stability of income through long-term employment is desirable. The lender will often perform ratio analysis when determining debt capacity.

Collateral

The amount of security or collateral that one can pledge to securitize their borrowing, will be a factor when determining the total amount that can be borrowed. Although collateral may make a loan safe it cannot make a loan sound.

Collateral is intended to induce the borrower to be orderly and timely in the re-payment of the loan since collateral is used for partial or full recovery if the borrower is unable to pay the loan according to its terms. Additionally, collateral is required to ensure that the borrower has a stake in the loan transaction.

Some types of collateral are considered better than others from a lender's perspective. Good quality collateral can come in many forms including equity in a home, or financial assets such as guaranteed investment certificates (GICs), Canada Savings Bonds (CSBs), or term deposits (TDs). Poor forms of collateral are personal assets like a stamp collection or jewelry, which have limited resale potential. A guarantor or co-signer who signs on a loan to provide support for the credit is equally responsible for the obligation and the re-payment of all debt. The assets held within RRSPs and RRIFs cannot be pledged as collateral for credit.

Capital

A lender is interested in a borrower's ability to repay the loan plus accrued interest in case of any unforeseen circumstances. Common occurrences that may require a capital injection include unemployment, illness, or a marital breakdown. Items that a lender would consider appropriate capital include investments and rental properties. A registered retirement savings plan (RRSP) is considered capital as individuals have saved in order to accumulate this capital sum and in an emergency, it can usually be redeemed. It is important to note that liquidating an RRSP will result in lowering net worth, and will incur income-tax withholding remittances.

Credit history

A borrower's credit history in the form of a credit report is used to evaluate the lender's risk.

The credit report, which is obtained from the local credit bureau, contains such information as the borrowers name, address, age, debts owed, employment/occupation, prior residential addresses and litigation details. Some information such as mortgage debt may not be listed in the credit reports as not all financial institutions share this debt history information with the credit bureau.

The credit bureau's members are area merchants and lending institutions that deal with consumer credit. Members are required to file information with the bureau. In return, these companies can refer to the credit bureau for information, as required. These members usually pay a user fee each time they access the credit bureau database. Since there is a time delay between when creditors report to the bureau and when the credit bureau actually records the transactions to the credit report, the bureau report may be out of date. Dun & Bradstreet produces similar reports for commercial lending purposes.

Danger signals which may indicate credit instability include the inability to meet past payment obligations, credit abuses, an applicant who lives beyond their means, no collateral, pending or prior lawsuits, a loan for a poor purpose, frequent job shifting, numerous inquiries to the credit bureau, frequent changing of residence and any lack of full disclosure to the lender.

Individuals can access their personal credit report by telephoning or visiting their local credit agency or bureau.

Types of credit

1. Mortgages

The largest financial commitment for most Canadians during their lifetime is the purchase of a home, and the subsequent mortgage commitments that homeownership entails. Therefore, it is imperative that purchasers educate themselves by studying and understanding mortgage features and restrictions.

The financial terms and conditions of a mortgage contract would include:

- the loan amount,
- interest rate,
- amortization period,
- loan to value ratio,
- term, and
- pre-payment privileges.

Each mortgage is a unique contract negotiated between the mortgagee (lender) and the mortgagor (borrower). It is prudent to review the mortgage contract with a financial advisor and a legal representative (lawyer or notary) **before** signing the document.

The mortgagee (lender):

- must be sure that the mortgagor holds clear title before the mortgage is arranged,
- must register the mortgage as security,
- must provide the mortgagor with the funds when needed, and
- must provide a discharge of the mortgage loan when certain circumstances arise.

The mortgagor (borrower) covenants to:

- make payments on time,
- pay the property taxes,
- insure the property,
- keep the property in good repair, and
- not sell the property without the mortgagee's written approval.

The loan to value ratio compares the loan amount to the value of the property for which the mortgage is made. A conventional mortgage has a loan to value ratio of 75% or less. This implies a down payment of at least 25% on a property that is purchased, and it means that the homebuyer therefore is borrowing less than 75% of the home's purchase price or appraised value.

A mortgage on a property for which the down payment is less than 25% is called a high ratio mortgage. A high ratio mortgage means that the loan to value ratio is more than 75% but less than 95%. A high ratio mortgage must be insured and this can be accomplished through Canada Mortgage and Housing Corporation (CMHC). CMHC requires all high ratio mortgages to be insured and the maximum insurable mortgage loan is 95% of the property's value. Borrower's may deal with their choice of a variety of lenders approved by CMHC in order to receive the CMHC insured mortgage. Approved lenders include most chartered banks, trust companies, credit unions, and life-insurance companies. CMHC will collect the insurance premium from the borrower and this insurance premium ensures that the lender will be fully repaid in the event of the borrowers default.

Amortization

Amortization is the length of time over which the loan, principal plus interest, will be fully repaid. Generally, the amortization period can be up to 25 years. Everything else being equal, the longer the amortization of the loan, the lower the required payment. One important financial planning consideration is to shorten the amortization of the mortgage (or any loan) in order to reduce the total interest costs paid to the lender and to build equity in the property as quickly as possible.

Term

Term refers to the length of time for which the lender will, according to the contract, advance the money and for which the interest rate on the mortgage is fixed. Mortgage terms typically vary from 6 months to 10 years. Generally speaking, the longer the term, the higher the interest rate. However, there have been occasions when the short-term interest rates have exceeded the long-term rates.

An open mortgage may be paid in whole or in part at any time and for this privilege, the interest rate is higher than on a closed mortgage. An open mortgage is appropriate when the borrower knows that they will be coming into additional funds, or if they plan to sell the home within a short period of time. An open mortgage would also be considered appropriate if interest rates were expected to fall. Generally speaking, open mortgages are of short duration, typically six months.

In contrast, a closed mortgage has its interest rate set, along with other fixed conditions, for the length of the mortgage term. A closed mortgage usually cannot be repaid in full before maturity without incurring interest penalties. Interest rates on closed mortgages are typically lower than the interest rates charged on comparable open mortgages. The advantage of a closed term mortgage is that the interest rate and payment are locked in for the chosen term. This provides the borrower with cash flow certainty and peace of mind.

Mortgage underwriting and the qualification process

A mortgage provides the lender with 2 types of security:

- the personal covenant of the mortgagor to re-pay and secondly,
- the security of the property that is being mortgaged.

With an owner occupied principal residence there will be no income generated, therefore the creditor is assessing the ability of the borrower to make and maintain all of the contracted financial commitments including the mortgage cost. The lender also assesses the value of the subject property and the character of the borrower as part of their decision-making process.

The assessment of character includes a review of creditworthiness. This is facilitated by a number of means:

(1) Credit application.

- A typical credit application will request details in terms of the amount of the loan requested and a statement of the purpose for the loan. The application will also provide details of the applicant e.g. name, age, address, employment, income, assets, liabilities, and ongoing expenses.
- Specifics are also required with respect to the legal description, address, location, and details of the property to be mortgaged.

- Credit applications typically contain a permission clause, which authorize the lender to contact references, verify employment, and to access the applicant's credit history.

(2) Credit analysis.

- The purpose of a credit analysis is to determine the borrower's ability and intention to fulfill the financial obligation. This analysis is facilitated by the use of financial data that is provided in the loan application and historical data, which is located in the credit report. Analysis of income, expenses, assets and liabilities is essential.

- Great importance is attached to confirming an applicant's annual gross income, since this value is critical in determining the maximum size of a mortgage or loan that can be prudently advanced by the lending institution.

(3) Appraisal of security.

- In order to determine the lending value of the underlying property, a professional appraiser provides an assessment of the property's current fair market value (FMV) for lending purposes.

- The appraisal of real estate uses three approaches: the cost approach, sales comparison approach, and the income approach to establish appraised values.

(4) Constraints to lending.

- A major constraint to any real estate lending decision is the loan to value ratio. The loan to value ratio establishes the owners net equity in a property. This ratio is based on the loan amount in proportion to the property's appraised value.

- A second major constraint is the ability of the mortgagor to service the debt. Potential borrowers are often overly optimistic regarding the size of the debt that they can carry. For this reason, lenders will factor into their debt servicing calculations, the additional costs of homeownership as well as purchase costs such as fees charged by CMHC, insurance premiums, appraisal fees, mortgage brokerage fees, land transfer taxes, GST, condominium fees and annual heating costs.

Mortgage Default

In the event of default on a mortgage agreement, the lender has the following remedies available:

(1) Sue on the personal covenants for non-performance,

(2) Take possession of the property,

(3) Exercise power of sale, or

(4) Foreclose title.

Power of sale

The mortgagee upon default on a mortgage agreement often seeks this remedy, because it is expedient. Since there is no court action involved and there is no statutory waiting period for the mortgagor to refinance, the procedure is quick and inexpensive. This option is most attractive in a stable or rising real estate market where the mortgagee can recover principal and interest. If the property is sold at a price above the amount owing, any remaining funds are paid to the mortgagor. If, after the sale, there is a deficiency, this deficiency is recoverable against the mortgagor.

Foreclosure

Under a mortgage foreclosure, the mortgagee sues for both possession and for payment. A foreclosure can involve a lengthy legal process. Foreclosure is pursued when it is worthwhile to own the property. Alternatively, foreclosure can be viewed as a powerful inducement to a mortgagor to keep current and not to allow payments to fall into arrears or the mortgage to default.

Mortgage jargon

Assumable. This mortgage feature allows a homebuyer to assume an existing mortgage on the purchased home. This can be an attractive selling feature if, for example, the mortgage carries an interest rate that is lower than the current market interest rate. Homebuyers will have to qualify to carry or assume the mortgage debt in order to release the vendor from the responsibility of the mortgage.

Convertible. mortgages can be converted at anytime into a longer-term mortgage, without fees or penalties. This feature is attractive if interest rates start to rise.

Portable. Some lenders allow the transfer of an existing mortgage to a new property, subject to certain qualifications. A portable mortgage is appropriate when the borrower has negotiated an attractive interest rate and wishes to maintain that interest rate.

Reverse mortgages can be arranged to provide homeowners with income from the equity they have accumulated in their residence. These plans, also called equity conversions, are sometimes referred to as a homeowner income plan. The process consists of a lender providing funds, secured by a mortgage, which are used to provide income to a homeowner. These income payments may be structured in such a fashion as to minimize or even eliminate income taxes. Upon death, this loan is repaid, often from a sale of the property. This type of financing can have dramatic impacts on the homeowner's estate. Reverse mortgages may work well for homeowners who are asset rich but cash poor, and do not wish to relocate, but nevertheless need to supplement their retirement income.

A **second mortgage** ranks behind a first mortgage in security. This higher credit risk on the part of the lender is usually reflected to the borrower through the use of a higher interest rate that is charged on the second mortgage.

Split term mortgages are a mix of any 2 or more mortgage terms in one mortgage product. The advantage of this option is that both an open and a closed term can be held within this one mortgage.

Variable-rate (VRM). The interest rate on this type of mortgage is re-adjusted according to a formula set out in the mortgage contract. Typically, interest on a VRM compounds monthly rather than compounding semiannually, as is the case of a conventional or high ratio mortgage. The interest rates are usually tied to the prime rate or to T-bills. Some VRMs set a cap on the maximum interest rate, or may limit any single adjustment. A VRM is very attractive when interest rates are declining and can in fact reduce the amortization period. Conversely, if interest rates are rising it is possible that payments may not be high enough to cover interest charges and the shortfall is added back to the principal.

Vendor take back is a mortgage provided by the vendor. This type of financing is sometimes set up as a second mortgage with commensurate higher interest rates. The vendor's motivation is typically to increase the appeal or saleability of the property.

Loans

Loans can be arranged such that they are either secured or unsecured by collateral. The risk in granting a loan from the lender's perspective determines the interest rate to be charged.

A promissory note is a form of unsecured loan. An unsecured, personal line of credit is a form of a signature loan. Without collateral, the security for unsecured loans is essentially character, integrity, and past credit performance.

A term, or installment loan, which is usually for a specific purpose, has an amortization schedule providing for regular payments. In the case of a fixed installment loan both the term and the interest rate are fixed and do not change over the term of the loan. In contrast, a variable loan carries an interest rate that floats, usually with the prime lending rate. A renewable loan has an interest rate, that is set for a period of time e.g. six months, at which point the loan renews at the current market interest rate. These types of loans are readily available at banks, trust companies, credit unions, and finance companies.

Demand loans are usually secured by collateral such as guaranteed investment certificates (GICs), Canada Savings Bonds (CSBs), term deposits (TDs), mutual funds, or other financial assets. Because the collateral is relatively liquid, demand loans generally carry a lower interest rate than other types of loans. The interest rate charged on a demand loan usually is not fixed and will vary with the prime lending rate. A demand loan can be pre-paid anytime without penalty. As the name suggests the lender, with 24-48 hours notice, can call a demand loan. A margin account at a brokerage firm is a good example of a demand loan.

Overdraft protection is generally short-term protection provided by a financial institution to cover short-term cash shortages. Usually, overdraft protection is attached to a checking account to prevent non-sufficient funds (NSF) charges.

Credit cards

There is a tremendous proliferation of easily available credit in the credit card market. One major contributing factor to the growth of credit is the securitization of asset-backed securities.

Credit cards are a form of revolving credit.

Interest charges and calculations vary from card to card. Some cards charge annual fees, while other credit cards include extras such as air mile travel benefits. There are substantial differences between bankcards and credit cards issued by retail outlets, and these should be researched before obtaining this type of credit.

4. Lines of credit

In recent years, the line of credit has evolved as a very popular and flexible financing option. A line of credit offers several advantages to consumers including:

- A credit limit, when approved, is available to be charged up or paid down at the holders whim.
- A line of credit can serve as a source of emergency funds.
- Credit can be accessed when the holder wishes to make a purchase or needs to access funds quickly.
- In some circumstances, when a line is paid down to zero there is no cost for keeping the credit line open.

The line of credit is a very flexible product and is suited to consumers who can prudently manage their own credit. There are 2 types of lines of credit, secured and unsecured. Credit lines can be secured by assets such as a home, stocks, or bonds. With collateral in place such as the above, a secured line of credit will usually bear a lower interest rate, as compared to an unsecured line.

5. Leasing

Essentially a lease allows a consumer (lessee) to rent a vehicle or other asset from a vendor (lessor) for a specified period of time at a particular cost. The lease payments cover financing costs, depreciation and other expenses that are incurred over the life of the asset.

Many individuals are strong supporters of leasing due to the perceived flexibility and low initial cash outlay that it provides. If a vehicle is needed for only half of its useful life, a lease can eliminate the time and effort required to dispose of the vehicle after it is no longer needed. Moreover, if technology will rapidly make an item obsolete e.g., a computer, a cancellable lease can protect the consumer.

A lease potentially provides a greater degree of financing since purchases financed by a loan typically require a down payment, or collateral, of 20% or more. Lenders are very reluctant to lend 100% of the cost for any item that is used as collateral. Therefore, the individual with a need but no cash may not be able to obtain the necessary financing. A lease provides an alternative way to consume today, with no equity commitment.

Leases, however, tend to cost more than loans. This is to be expected considering the risk and return issues. Certainly, the leasing company (lessor) bears more risk than a creditor, because the lessor bears all of the normal risks of ownership, such as establishing that insurance is maintained. Further, while the consumer (lessee) has more flexibility to avoid technological obsolescence, the lessor charges a higher rent because they now bear that risk. The same is true with respect to 100% financing. The potential loss due to default is greater to a lessor than to a lender of other types of credit because there is no collateral with which to absorb losses in the event of repossession.

In some circumstances, leasing may be more efficient. Consider the family that needs 2 cars. If they lease the vehicles, they may pay more for them than if they bought them outright, but they might get a service contract with the lease. The leasing company may be willing to give a discount on service, in order to get the lease.

Who owns the property at the end of the lease? Unless it is specified in the lease contract, the property belongs to the lessor. The lessor stands to gain from any increase in the value of the property. Frequently, this right of ownership upon termination of the lease is given to the lessee for "free". In such leases, the monthly lease payments are higher than they would normally have to be if the lessor retained the ownership of the property.

None of these considerations provides absolute support for leasing. There are some benefits for the lessee, but they tend to raise the risk to the lessor, who therefore charges a higher price. Clearly, by adding a go between instead of buying directly, the additional party must earn a profit and this profit must come from the lease payments.

The advantages of using Leverage

Leverage refers to using borrowed funds (debt) to finance the purchase and ownership of assets, to magnify the return on investment. Leverage is often measured by the debt/equity ratio. The debt to equity ratio is calculated as total debt (current debt plus long-term debt) divided by net worth.

The use of debt imposes fixed and legally enforceable recurring costs, on a borrower. When an investor borrows (employs leverage) to make an investment, the loan increases the potential variation of yields on the equity portion of the investment. If the investment rises in value and the investor re-pays the loan, the resulting return on equity is enhanced. On the other hand, if the investment were to fall in value and then the investment is sold to repay the loan, the resulting loss on equity is exaggerated. In other words, leverage can be a double edged sword, it can work either for or against the investor.

Crunching the Numbers: The Lender's Tools

All lenders are concerned with a debtor's ability to re-pay the loan. The ability to re-pay any loan depends upon a number of factors including existing debt obligations and current uncommitted cash flow.

- **Debt burden** or debt service measures the percentage of income spent servicing debt. Debt burden equals total debt divided by income.

- **Gross debt service ratio (GDSR)** calculates the percentage of gross annual income that a borrower spends on basic housing costs. Homeowner mortgage payments, property taxes, annual heating costs, and 50% of condominium fees are divided by gross annual income. As a rule of thumb, GDSR should not exceed the range of 30% to 32% of gross annual income.

- **Total debt service ratio (TDSR)** calculates the percentage of gross annual income that a borrower spends servicing their total debt. TDSR includes housing costs mentioned above plus all other debt payments. A creditor will normally factor in an allowance for any available, even though unused, pre-existing credit facility. As a rule of thumb, total debt should not exceed 40% of gross annual income.

- **Debt to asset ratio** or the **debt ratio** is a measure of creditor protection. The debt ratio is calculated as total debt divided by total assets. The reciprocal of the debt ratio i.e. total assets divided by total debt is called asset coverage.

- **Liquidity** describes the ability to meet debt service, and other fixed payments in the short term.

- **Current ratio** measures the ability to meet short-term obligations with short-term assets. The current ratio equals total current assets divided by total current liabilities and is a very important liquidity measure.

- **Working capital** measures excess liquidity. Working capital equals total current assets minus total current liabilities. Excess liquidity may be viewed negatively because it indicates that there are idle funds that could be more productively allocated to other areas earning higher rates of return on the investment.

- **Solvency** describes 2 different measures of financial strength:

    1. The ability to pay debts as they come due, and

2. The excess of assets over liabilities, and therefore a positive value for net worth.

Tips for dealing effectively with lenders

- It is important to remember that being granted credit **is not a right, it must be earned!**
- Go prepared to the interview.
- Be realistic. Know how much will be required, why, and when it is needed.
- Ask questions of the lender. Ensure that all covenants and conditions of the loan are understood.
- Be honest. Never surprise the lender.
- Be positive.
- Be prepared to offer security or collateral.
- Understand the risk components. Creditors will always seek to minimize risk.
- Negotiate effectively. Know beforehand the amount of debt that can be supported by affordable, regular, monthly payments; and approximately, how large a monthly payment can be afforded.

Debt management strategies

- Financial advisors recommend that borrowers use credit wisely. Read the fine print located in the credit documents carefully and be certain to understand how the interest rates are calculated.
- Pre-arrange credit facilities before they are needed through prudent financial planning. This ensures that the most favourable interest rates will be available when needed.
- Credit is not a right, and it must be controlled and deployed efficiently in order to maximize wealth.
- Avoid unnecessary service charges and any hidden fees, which increase the effective interest rate.
- Reduce non-deductible debt. The *Income Tax Act* restricts the deductibility of certain interest charges.

- Pay off highest interest rate debt first. The contract fine print contains detail on the method used for interest rate calculations and the rates to be charged.
- Reposition assets. Sell non-productive assets. Re-structure portfolios to maximize after-tax efficiency. Careful restructuring might allow what previously had been non-deductible debt interest payments into a deductible interest expense for income tax purposes.
- Match borrowing term to purpose. Finance long-term investments and pay current consumption from cash flow.
- Negotiate a repayment plan with creditors.
- Consolidate high interest rate revolving debts (credit cards) to a lower rate loan with a single fixed re-payment schedule to provide for manageable cashflows. Any additional free cash flow generated by this strategy should be used to further reduce the debt's amortization period.

Signs of approaching trouble

- Thinking that declaring bankruptcy will solve debt re-payment problems.
- Refusing to deal with the problem in the hope that it will go away.
- Persistent telephone calls from creditors.
- High percentage of net worth "invested" in personal use assets e.g. furniture.
- Using credit facilities to create or generate income.
- Postponing or stalling debt repayments.
- Few assets or savings; low net worth.
- No clear idea of one's level of expenditure or cash flow.
- Spending more time shopping for a new sofa than for investments e.g. RRSP's.
- Frequently taking advances against future pay cheques.
- Eagerly awaiting the next credit card to arrive in the mail.
- New monthly credit charges exceed monthly payments.
- Arranging new credit that is used to pay existing debts.

- Continuously arguing with a spouse about finances.
- Expenses exceeding income.
- Borrowing from one credit card to pay off another.
- Using retirement or emergency funds to pay for current consumption.
- Unable to make minimum required payments.
- Spending paycheque earnings before they are received.

Glossary

Asset. Something that an individual or business owns.

Asset Backed Security (ABS). A security similar to a mortgage-backed security. A pool of asset backed securities. These pools of assets can consist of auto loans (CARs), credit card loans (CARDs), computer leases, small-business loans, or truck leases.

Bankable loan. Loan considered by the creditor to be of acceptable risk, and which carries a commensurate return.

Bankrupt. The legal status of an individual or company that is insolvent and whose assets a trustee therefore administers for its creditors in bankruptcy.

Blended payment. A loan or mortgage payment of a fixed dollar amount and which is composed of both principal and interest combined. Because the payment is the same each month, the principal portion of the loan is reduced with each successive payment.

Chattel. Personal property as opposed to real property. When chattels are used as collateral the resulting document evidencing debt is called a chattel mortgage.

Collateral. Money or property pledged as security for a loan.

Condition. A term within a contract that if breached, may cancel the contract. Debtors must fulfill conditions.

Covenant. A written promise, restriction, or other agreement contained within a contract.

Creditworthiness. The ability to repay debts based upon past history, future prospects, and other criteria.

Debt ratio. Measures the degree of financing provided by creditors. Calculated as total debt divided by total assets.

Debt service. The regular payments of principal, interest, and any other included costs made on a loan.

Demand loan. A loan on which a financial institution can demand full repayment, at anytime.

Discharging the mortgage. When the mortgage is repaid in full, and the lender no longer has a claim on the property, the mortgage is discharged by removing the lien.

Fixed charge coverage. A leverage ratio calculated as earnings divided by fixed expenses.

Foreclosure. A legal process undertaken by a lender to obtain possession of a property, because of the mortgagor's default in payment of the mortgage debt.

High ratio mortgage. A loan whose balance exceeds 75% of the lending value of a property.

Insolvent. A term describing a person or firm whose liabilities are greater than its assets. A firm or person with the inability to meet and pay current debts as they come due is also said to be insolvent.

Lease. A contract which provides for the use of, but not the ownership of an asset.

Lessee. The consumer who assumes a lease.

Lessor. The party that grants a lease.

Leverage ratios. Measure the degree to which creditors have provided financing.

Lien.A legal claim or charge, on real or personal property for the payment of a debt or liability.

Line of credit. Funds provided by a creditor up to a predetermined maximum, and which are typically payable on demand.

Liquidity crisis. A term describing temporary insolvency. The inability to meet fixed obligations when due. This occurs when short-term liabilities exceed short-term assets.

Loan ratio. Compares the loan amount to the value of the property for which the loan is made.

Margin account. A brokerage account for which collateral is posted by the investor. The initial margin is the deposit required at origination, while the maintenance margin is the minimum collateral necessary at all times.

Mortgage. Document evidencing a debt owed by the borrower (mortgagor) to the lender (mortgagee). Mortgages can have a number of different forms, which revolve around title to the property. Registration of the mortgage transfers the mortgagor's interest in land to the mortgagee, as security for the repayment of the debt.

Mortgagee. The lender.

Mortgagor. The borrower.

Mortgage-backed security (MBS) is a share in a pool of residential mortgages, for which the principal and interest payments pass through to shareholders. Income is paid to MBS holders, usually monthly.

Prime rate. The interest rate established by each financial institution. This is the rate usually charged to the financial institution's best customers.

Principal. The amount of the loan.

Securitization. The process by which pools of assets are transformed into negotiable and marketable securities.

Title. The formal, legal document that conveys the right to ownership of property.

Questions

1) How difficult is it to obtain financing?

Obtaining financing can be relatively easy, if there is a history with the financing company, strong credit, good net worth and collateral available, if required. When one or more of these factors are missing, the difficulty in receiving credit will increase. Financing of any type is difficult to obtain if an individual has a poor credit history.

2) A borrower requires some financing advice. Who can supply this?

It will depend upon what type of advice is required. Details of a general nature may be obtained from a financial advisor, accountant, or lawyer. Specific advice regarding qualifications for financing and product details should be requested directly from the lender.

3) Why is a good banking relationship important?

A good banking relationship is important for 2 reasons:

- A lender will use the banking history as a factor in underwriting the credit application and in making financial decisions about granting credit, and
- A good relationship with the financial institution may open some doors to providing the borrower with credit or a preferred interest rate.

Individuals seeking credit should approach their primary financial institution first for these credit requests before requesting funding from sources that have no knowledge of the individual.

4) What should a borrower do if they cannot meet their debt payments?

If a borrower is unable to meet their debt payments, they should proactively contact their credit grantor to discuss the options that may be available to them. Most lenders are willing to work with debtors to determine what alternatives, if any, exist. Withholding information from creditors and not being forthcoming may destroy any goodwill established with the lender.

5) Why would a financial institution decline a credit request?

The credit request may be declined for numerous reasons including poor credit history, damaged character, insufficient collateral, low net worth, the lack of capital to pay off debt in the event of payment default, and for the inability to support the new credit being applied for, as well as any existing debt payments currently required.

6) How does the use of leverage affect the cost of borrowing?

Leverage is the use of borrowed funds to finance the purchase of assets. If borrowed funds are used to purchase income-producing investments then, as a general rule, the interest cost on the borrowed funds is deductible for income tax purposes subject to Revenue Canada's qualifications.

The income-tax deductibility of interest effectively reduces the cost of borrowing. For example, the after-tax cost of a 7.5% deductible investment loan to an investor in the 40% tax bracket is:

$7.5 \times (1 - \text{tax rate}) = 7.5 \times (0.6) = 4.5\%$. Leverage can therefore magnify the after-tax return on investment that is particularly evident when the investment produces a rate of return that is greater than the cost of borrowing.

The use of leverage to purchase investment assets can be viewed as a method by which the investor can manufacture or create a tax shelter.

7) Why does the financial institution require security/collateral?

The lender may request collateral if any one of these C's of credit are missing i.e., character, capacity, capital, or credit history. The collateral provides a level of comfort to the lender that should the credit fall into arrears or default, the debt can be repaid through liquidation of the collateral.

8) How does a borrower effectively negotiate with their banker?

Effective negotiation is an art but it can be learned by employing a few basic principles. Some tips to consider when negotiating for credit are:

- Do not try to hold the lender hostage. For example, "you give me this or I'll do this".
- Do your homework. Be aware of credit details, current interest rates, collateral available etc.
- Be reasonable. Be willing to give as well as take.
- Use correct facts and information.

Financing Ratios

Where:

PIT = Mortgage Principal + Interest + Property Taxes

Gross Debt Service Ratio

$$\text{GDSR} = \frac{\text{PIT + Heating + 50\% Condo Fees}}{\text{Gross Annual Income}}$$

Total Debt Service Ratio

$$\text{TDSR} = \frac{\text{PIT + Heating + 50\% Condo Fees + Other Debt}}{\text{Gross Annual Income}}$$

$$\text{Debt Burden} = \frac{\text{Total Debt}}{\text{Annual Income}}$$

CHAPTER 3

Insurance and Risk Management

Building net worth over a lifetime requires prudent planning and the implementation of sound strategies. The planning process should include each of the following steps:

- the establishment and analysis of goals,
- a review of the current financial situation and the various opportunities and/or problems facing the individual including an insurance needs analysis directed to attain the goals, and

- involvement of a qualified professional to provide tax, investment and estate planning expertise.

Insurance may be defined as a contract in which one person pays money, which is called a premium, to a second party, known as the insurer, who promises to reimburse the individual for **specified losses**, should these losses occur. Insurance is a way to distribute losses and eliminate uncertainty. Insurance can be thought of as the reverse of gambling.

One of the basic principles of insurance is that of indemnity. Indemnification simply comprises compensation to an insured, such that he or she is in the same financial position after a loss, as they enjoyed before the loss occurred. Note that it is not intended for insured individuals to profit from an insurance settlement.

The concept of insurance is relatively simple. People who face potential losses band together to establish a fund with which to compensate those who actually experience disaster. The principle of risk sharing is applied when large numbers of people pay a regular fee, which is known and therefore certain, in exchange for protection against a hazard that is uncertain.

The premium paid by individuals is composed of the pure cost of insurance plus a loading charge, with the loading charge representing the insurer's costs including a profit.

The pure cost of insurance is dependent upon three factors:

- the probability of the event occurring,
- the cost of the compensation, and
- the number of individuals sharing the risk.

Insurance planning is essentially a risk management activity. Risk management can be defined as the assessment of the size of a potential loss and the probability of its occurrence.

The 5 steps in the risk management process include:

(1) The identification of potential risks,

(2) The evaluation of the risks,

(3) The controlling of the risks,

(4) The financing of the risks, and

(5) Monitoring of the risk profile.

There are a number of methods of handling or managing risk. The most common methods include:

Risk avoidance.

Risk avoidance simply means that an individual can evade certain risks merely by staying away from the risk that one chooses not to incur. For example, an individual will not die in a plane crash if the individual chooses not to fly. An individual will not be arrested for drunk driving, if the individual does not drink and drive.

Risk reduction.

The reduction of risk involves some positive action that is taken. Common examples of risk reduction would include the installation of dead bolt locks, or the use of smoke detectors in a home.

Risk retention.

The retention of risk means that an individual chooses to self-fund any losses that may be incurred. For example, an individual may chose a deductible of $1,000 on their automobile insurance coverage. This indicates that the individual is prepared to personally pay the first $1,000 of damage incurred in an auto accident.

Risk transfer.

The transfer of risk simply means that individuals who are unable, or unwilling, to bear a particular loss may transfer this uncertainty to a third party, usually an insurance company, who is prepared to accept the risk. Risk transfer is the most common method of managing large risks and this is the topic of the current chapter.

Not all risks are insurable and insurance companies only deal with those that are. The factors determining an insurable risk include:

- the loss must be definable and quantifiable,
- the loss must be accidental, or occur as a result of chance events,
- the loss must be large enough to cause financial hardship, and
- the cost of insuring must be economically feasible.

Additionally, an insurable interest must exist. Insurable interest is a person's real financial interest in an object or in another person.

Types of life insurance coverage

There are many reasons why an individual would have life insurance, including the desire to:

- create an estate for the heirs before one has the opportunity to accumulate an estate,
- supplement the existing estate,
- payoff outstanding debts,
- pay estate settlement costs such as legal or probate fees,
- protect an individual's business interests or investments, and to
- create a charitable donation.

Life insurance for many people tends to be a very confusing subject. This confusion arises because a few basic types of policies have been expanded upon and elaborated with special features and which have a bewildering variety of names. There is no apparent standardization and these names vary among each of the many life insurance companies licensed to do business in Canada.

Life insurance can be either term insurance or permanent insurance. All other forms of life insurance are variations of either term or permanent.

Life insurance policies are based on mortality tables. Mortality tables are used, by actuaries, to calculate life expectancy's or the probability of dying. A mortality table is based on an original hypothetical cohort of 100,000 individuals and for each year after birth, a calculation of how many of the 100,000 in the original cohort are still alive and how many have died during the year. Mortality tables exist for males and females. Since the probability of any individual dying increases every year, the pure cost of life insurance coverage increases with age.

The pure cost of life insurance coverage for any specific age can be closely approximated by calculating the insurance policy death benefit times the annual mortality rate. For example, assuming a mortality rate of 0.28% for a 45-year-old male requiring an insurance policy of $500,000, the premium is equal to $500,000 times 0.0028 = $1,400. The premium for the following year, assuming a mortality rate that rises to 0.30% for a 46 year old male, would amount to $1,500. Moreover, by age 50, at which time the mortality rate has grown to 0.45%, the annual pure cost of insurance would increase to $2,250.

Term insurance.

Term insurance is also known as pure insurance. Term insurance has no cash or savings value included within the policy and is the simplest type of life insurance to understand for most people. As the name suggests, term insurance protects for a limited and specified time i.e. the term. The term can vary from one year to age 100. There are many variations of term insurance available to Canadians.

The most basic type of term insurance is known as annual guaranteed renewable term (ART). ART is typically found in a group insurance policy provided by many employers to their employees. An annual guaranteed renewable term policy would rise in price each year (at renewal) as the insured ages. Guaranteed renewable means that coverage will continue in effect, until the end of the term, without having to undergo further medical underwriting qualification, as long as the insured agrees to pay the increased premium. An annual renewable term policy is the most cost-effective method of purchasing life insurance coverage for a short period, since the pure cost of insurance is recalculated and increases each year. A disadvantage of ART is that it becomes prohibitively expensive for an older individual.

At the opposite end of the spectrum from ART with its annually increasing premiums, is level premium term insurance. Level premium term insurance, as the name suggests, carries a premium which is unchanging. By necessity, level premium term insurance must charge premiums that are higher in the early years than ART, and lower than the premiums charged for ART at later ages. It is possible to purchase level premium term insurance for terms to age 65, age 75, or to age 100.

In between these 2 extremes, term insurance policies are often described as step term. Step term policies are the most common type of term insurance policies that are encountered in the Canadian term insurance marketplace. Step term policies typically have a premium which is level for some specified time. The most common, are policies with premiums that are level for 5 or 10 years. If the policyholder decides to keep the policy (renew it), then premiums are adjusted upward and remain level for another 5 or 10 years at which point the premiums rise again and are fixed for another 5 or 10-year period. An individual can purchase 5-year term to age 65. The policy expires when the insured reaches age 65 i.e. coverage ends. Also commonly available are 10-year renewal step term policies to age 75.

Decreasing term insurance requires the payment of a premium; however, under this type of term insurance the death benefits reduce over time.

An example of decreasing term insurance is called mortgage insurance. As a mortgage is repaid, over time the outstanding principal balance declines, as does the death benefit. It is important to note that a policy with a decreasing death benefit combined with a level premium means that the pure cost of coverage per $1,000 of death benefit must be rising.

Most term insurance policies offered in the Canadian marketplace are guaranteed renewable; however, a review of the policy declaration sheet can quickly confirm this. The declaration sheet will also delineate the maximum premiums that are required to be paid at each renewal. Insurance companies cannot charge more than this maximum premium but for example, due to favorable mortality experience, the insurer may charge less than this amount.

Additionally, most term insurance policies contain a convertibility feature. Convertibility allows the insured to convert a term insurance policy, without having to medically re-qualify for coverage, into another policy that is usually a type of permanent insurance offered by the same insurance company. The convertibility feature will usually contain restrictions such that the conversion feature must be exercised before some specified date, such as age 60.

Conversion of an existing term policy might be advantageous to an individual who requires permanent life insurance coverage but who can no longer qualify for a new policy due to poor health.

Permanent insurance

Permanent insurance usually contains a savings component in addition to the life insurance death benefit.

(a) Whole life

The premiums payable on a whole life policy are usually level for the lifetime of the insured. The level premium means that the insured is over paying the pure cost of coverage in the early years and conversely, under paying the pure cost of life insurance coverage in later years. This overpayment of the premium is retained and invested by the insurance company and forms the policy reserves. The reserves ensure that the insurance company is able to continue coverage in the later years due to an underpayment of premium as the life insured ages and the pure cost of insurance rises. The reserve is owned and controlled by the insurance company. If an insured individual cancels this type of policy, they will receive the cash surrender value (CSV) of the policy, which is usually some percentage of the reserve. The CSV of the policy is guaranteed under the terms of the contract and is found in the declaration sheet of all whole life policies.

(b) **Universal Life (UL)**

Universal life insurance (UL) was originally introduced into the Canadian marketplace in the early 1980s. UL is a contract that allows the policyholder flexibility. Universal life insurance combines term insurance, in case of the insured's premature death, with a tax-deferred savings component. The insurance companies offer a wide variety of investment options for the savings component of the UL policy and these cash values may be creditor protected. Additionally, cash values plus the face value of the term policy can be paid tax-free to the beneficiaries as a death benefit. Cash accumulating life insurance policies would not usually be set up as holdings within an RRSP or RRIF.

Universal life policies are purchased for the death benefits. An equity-based UL policy may provide a gain due to capital appreciation. Investors anticipating high inflation and rising interest rates would not choose a UL policy whose investment component is based upon fixed income bonds but might instead select one that is based upon equity markets, or one that is money-market oriented. Most UL policies permit switching between stock, bond, and money-market indices to provide for maximum flexibility.

Premiums vary widely with the type of underlying term insurance policy and with such factors as the age, sex, and health status of the life insured. Premiums include the pure cost of insurance, sales commissions, and insurance company operating profits. Some policies have penalties for cancellation before specified dates.

Policies can be fully paid up for life in as few as seven years, depending upon the contract purchased. UL policies may provide some inflation protection through their adjustable death benefits. Policies can also be cancelled and cash values claimed at any time. Accumulated premiums plus investment income performance determine the policy's cash value. However, the actual payments of cash values may require several weeks of processing time. It is strongly recommended that new insurance policies be in place before existing policies are cancelled.

Life insurance policies do not trade on a secondary market.

In addition to the WebSite of the Canadian Life and Health Insurance Association (CLHIA), many of the Canadian insurance companies maintain their own WebSite's. A great deal of information is available and may be obtained by visiting these WebSites.

Life insurance regulation and risk

Insurance companies are regulated by the Office the Superintendent Financial Institutions (OSFI) federally, and by the provincial Superintendents of Insurance.

Risks faced by policyholders include:

- Policies that provide for market returns on cash value investments also carry market risk.
- A UL policy invested in a bond fund would lose cash value if interest rates rose, while one invested in stocks would lose in an equity market downturn. Policies that invest cash value in fixed income instruments, for example, are less subject to fluctuating income and reinvestment risk than a policy invested in money-market instruments.
- The Canada Deposit Insurance Corporation (CDIC) does not insure life insurance cash values. The Compensation Corporation (CompCorp) covers life insurance companies in Canada. Canadian life insurance companies are rated by services such as TRAC, DBRS, Standard & Poor's, and Moody's.

The insurance contract

All types of insurance contracts tend to follow a similar template.

- **The preamble or declaration sheet.** This page outlines information such as who is covered, the effective dates, the premiums to be paid, and the risks to be covered.
- **The insuring agreement.** In this section, details are provided as to the property to be covered and the perils against which coverage is provided. Important paragraphs in this section include the policy's exclusions and limitations. Is important that these limitations and exclusions be fully understood.
- **The statutory conditions.** These paragraphs are required by law (see below).
- **The policy conditions.** This section indicates what an insured must do in order to have coverage continue. The policy conditions state

what the insured must do in case of loss and how the insured may recover after suffering a loss.

- **The signature clauses.** Insurance policies are signed and witnessed in this area.
- **Riders or endorsements.** These are modifications or amendments to the contract. Riders or endorsements are always appended to the contract and form part of the contract.
- **Application Form.** A copy of the original application for life and disability insurance is attached to the policy.

Statutory or standard life insurance policy provisions

Some of the more common life insurance policy provisions that are required by provincial statutes typically include:

(1) **Incontestable clause.** After a policy has been in force for 2 years the life insurance company, except in the case of fraud or the intentional misstatement of health status, cannot contest a claim.

(2) **Grace period.** The specified time usually 30 or 31 days, after which a premium is due, that an insurance policy's protection will remain in force. The overdue premium may be repaid and no penalty is applied if paid within the grace period.

(3) **Reinstatement.** After a life insured has complied with the conditions stipulated in the policy, a lapsed policy can be restored to an in force and premium paying condition. The insured will usually have to submit to medical underwriting in order to reinstate the policy, and pay all of the back premiums plus interest. Typically, a lapsed policy can be reinstated within a 2-year period.

(4) **Suicide clause.** Most life insurance policies deny claims, other than the return of premiums paid, for death by suicides within the first 2 years that the policy is in force.

(5) **Ownership Loan provisions.** Typically, the policyholder can arrange for a loan from the insurance company up to the cash value of the policy. The interest rate that is to be charged on the loan and the method of its calculation will be stated within the policy.

(6) **Non-forfeiture options.** These are the options, other than surrender, that are available to a policy that has accumulated cash value upon the policy's termination. The cash value may be used to purchase a reduced death benefit, paid up cash value policy. Alternatively, the cash value may be used to purchase extended term insurance.

(7) **Settlement options.** Life insurance policies typically allow for several optional methods of receiving death benefits. The most common settlement options are: the receipt of a fixed amount each month until the proceeds are exhausted, a fixed period option which pays over a fixed time, or a life income option.

(8) **Dividends.** A policy that participates in the profitability of the insurance company may pay dividends. Policy dividends are not guaranteed and may be thought of as a rebate of overpaid premiums. The policyholder will have a choice as to how dividends are to be paid. Typically, the policyholder is allowed to receive the dividend as cash, apply the dividend against premiums due, leave the dividend with the insurance company to accumulate interest, use the dividend to purchase one year term insurance, or use the dividend to purchase additional paid up cash value coverage.

(9) **Conversion.** Typically contained in group insurance or term insurance policy. This clause allows the insured to convert to a permanent insurance policy issued by the underwriting insurer, within a limited time that is specified in the contract. The insured is not required to supply evidence of insurability when the conversion clause is exercised. The premiums paid for the permanent policy will be based on the insured's attained age.

Life insurance policy riders include:

1. **Accidental death.** Provides extra coverage, typically equal to the death benefit of the original policy hence the name double indemnity. Benefits are paid if death is by accidental means.

2. **Disability waiver of premiums.** This rider states that after a qualifying period specified in the contract, a totally disabled policy owner will not be required to pay premiums in order to have the life insurance remain in force.

3. **Guaranteed insurability.** This rider allows the policyholder to increase insurance coverage, at pre-specified future times, without having to supply further evidence of insurability.
4. **Term rider.** This rider allows the addition of a term insurance policy to a permanent insurance policy.

Disability insurance (DI)

The most valuable asset that the vast majority of the adult population owns is their ability to wake-up each morning, and to go to work in order to create net worth and to earn the current income required to provide for a reasonable lifestyle. Without this ability, a great many Canadians would be in dire straits. There is a great deal of information which is readily available regarding life insurance and the choices that are available, and even more opinions and information regarding the appropriate choice of life insurance coverage in a given situation. More importantly however, research studies show that the probability of a significant period of disability is much higher than the probability of death at any given age up to normal retirement at age 65. Studies also point out that more than half of all disabilities exceed one year in duration. In fact, disability insurance and the continuing ability or inability to go to work in order to pay the bills is of far greater consequence than life insurance considerations for most working Canadians.

Factors which affect the cost of private disability insurance (DI) coverage

The enforcement of disability claims is a matter of interpreting the disability insurance contract clauses. It is therefore particularly important when considering or evaluating disability insurance coverage that individuals understand the major terms and conditions of the disability insurance policy contract, which affect the premiums paid.

(1) **Guaranteed renewable and noncancellable contract.** A disability insurance policy should be guaranteed renewable and noncancellable. If the policy is not guaranteed renewable and noncancellable, the insurer can cancel the insurance at their option, or, at renewal, they can require additional or increased premiums. Any policy that is cancellable and not guaranteed renewable will certainly be less expensive than a guaranteed, renewable, noncancellable disability insurance contract

(2) **The definition of total disability.** There are many definitions of total disability contained within various DI contracts. The 2 most basic definitions are "own occupation" and "any occupation".

Under an "any occupation" definition if the insured has the ability to work at another job or occupation, then they will not qualify to receive benefits. If, on the other hand, an individual has a contract with an " own occupation" definition, and they cannot work at that occupation or job, they are entitled to receive benefits. It is therefore critical that individuals understand the definition of disability contained within their own policy contract. These simplistic definitions are included merely for illustrative purposes, and serve to reinforce the requirement to carefully review the basic definitions before purchasing DI coverage. As a rule of thumb, the definition of disability has the greatest effect on DI premiums. Therefore, everything else being equal, given 2 apparently identical DI policies, one which costs $500 per year and the other which costs $1,000 per year, look first at the definition of disability and next to the policy limitations and exclusions.

(3) **The elimination period.** The elimination period is the time that must elapse after a covered disability occurs before benefit payments begin. Generally, the shorter the waiting period, the higher the premium. The elimination period is a form of deductible or self-insurance in that the longer an insured individual is prepared to self fund i.e. not receive any benefits, the less expensive the premium will be. Benefits can start as early as 15 days, or they can be deferred for as long as 2 years. Benefits are typically paid 30 days in arrears. Note that an individual, who owns a policy with a 30 day elimination period, does not receive a benefit check on the 30th day, but after 60 days. Benefits are received on a policy with a 90-day elimination period after 120 days.

(4) **The maximum benefit period.** The maximum benefit period is the length of time for which benefits are payable to the insured. Some policies will pay benefits for a maximum of 2 years, others for 5 years, and the best policies pay to age 65.

(5) **The maximum benefit amount.** All else being equal, the higher the maximum benefits payable, the higher the premium. There will be restrictions imposed by each insurance company that will limit coverage to a specified percentage of pre-disability earnings. Each insurance company will also have an overall maximum dollar benefit that can be paid to an insured.

(6) **Occupation.** Certain occupations are far more prone to injury that others. White-collar professionals tend to be considered as low-risk occupations vs. blue-collar occupations. Certain occupations,

which are considered dangerous or otherwise risky, may be excluded from coverage altogether by the insurance company.

(7) **Age.** Disability insurance premiums rise with age.

(8) **Hobbies.** Persons engaging in dangerous hobbies, for example, rock climbing or mountain climbing can expect to pay higher premiums.

(9) **Exclusions and limitations.** A policy with fewer exclusions or limitations will carry a higher premium than a policy with many limitations and/or exclusions. Note that limitations and exclusions might limit or exclude coverage for persons who have pre-existing medical conditions.

(10) **Partial Disability.** Typically, in order to receive benefits an individual must be totally disabled; however, it is not unusual for a physician to encourage an individual to return to work as quickly as possible, even on a part-time basis. Note that if the contract requires total disability on the part of the insured and the individual is able to work part-time, they are not totally disabled. They are only partially disabled and do not qualify for benefits. It is therefore very important to recognise and consider either purchasing a rider that allows payments of partial disability benefit or alternatively the purchase of a DI contract which already includes in the policy contract itself the ability to receive partial disability benefits.

Critical illness insurance

Statistics show that Canadians are surviving critical illnesses such as cancer more frequently now than in prior years. Improvements in medicine and medical treatments have resulted in promising prognosis' for many illnesses. However, the occurrence of critical illnesses is on the increase, and the facts indicate that approximately one out of every 2 Canadian men and one of every three Canadian women will encounter a critical illness during their lifetime.

Maintaining a similar quality of life after the diagnosis of a critical illness and dealing with financial commitments can cause hardship for individuals and their families. Critical illness insurance can protect a family's future. Generally, critical illness insurance will help to the pay off a debt, for example a mortgage, or to help provide funds that can be used for medical treatment in the event that one falls victim to specific illnesses including stroke, cancer, or heart attack.

Property loss insurance

The majority of Canadians will be affected by personal property, home, and auto insurance policy decisions at some point during their lifetime.

Property insurance

Property insurance includes insurance coverage for the risk of damage to personal property resulting from flood, fire, or vandalism. The most important personal assets for most Canadians that require property insurance coverage are their homes and automobiles. However, property insurance can be purchased to insure furnishings, clothing, appliances, boats, or collectibles. It is usually recommended that personal property, furnishings and collectibles be listed and described separately, and that any master list including photographs be stored outside of the insured property, in a safety deposit box for example.

Typically, property insurance coverage is either "specified perils" or "all risks". "Specified perils" provides protection only against those perils named specifically in the contract. An "all risks" policy is not limited to perils that are specifically named in the policy. The "all risks" policy, because of its wider coverage, is more expensive than the rather limited coverage provided by "specified perils" policies.

Homeowners insurance

A home is one of the largest purchases most people make during their lifetime. Therefore, homeowners insurance protection is prudent and strongly recommended. Usually, a homeowners policy covers damage to the home, out buildings (e.g. garage), contents, and injuries to a third party suffered on the property.

(1) Valuation of property.

Home insurance can be purchased for replacement value or depreciated actual value coverage. Replacement value can be described as the replacement of property with a new or comparable item and for this coverage, a higher insurance premium will be charged. Depreciated property coverage on the other hand, compensates the insured for the actual value of the property, considering its age and condition.

(2) Policy deductibles.

The deductible is the portion that must be paid by the insured party before the insurance company will make any payment.

Higher deductibles will usually mean lower insurance premiums because:

(a) The insured shares in part of the loss,

(b) The insured is encouraged to settle their own small losses, and

(c) The deductible is an incentive for the insured to avoid situations that may result in loss or damage.

(3) Third party liability insurance.

This coverage protects homeowners, up to a specified limit, should a third party be injured while on the property.

Some of the factors to consider when purchasing this insurance include:

- the state of repair of the property,
- whether the homeowner has pets on the premises,
- the types of activities carried on at the home, e.g., a swimming pool,
- the appropriate amount of coverage to cover losses. Generally, the minimum third party liability coverage recommended is $1 million.

(4) Types of homeowners insurance policies.

(a) Fire insurance. Protects in case of fire, lightning, smoke damage, and other similar and specifically listed perils.

(b) Tenant's or Renter's policies. These policies are purchased by renters, should their personal property such as furniture be damaged or lost. Typically, the renters policy also covers third party liability. It does not cover the building structure, since that is the landlord's property.

(c) Comprehensive. This is the most common type of homeowners policy, and typically covers the building, contents, and third party liability. Comprehensive policies can be tailored to meet individual circumstances.

Automobile and vehicle insurance

Vehicle insurance has various elements including property damage coverage, liability coverage including the death or injury of a third party, collision coverage, and comprehensive coverage. The various provincial legislatures require that the registered owners of an automobile or vehicle carry certain minimum insurance coverage's.

(1) **Liability coverage.**

Liability insurance coverage includes the injury, death, or damages to the property of another party. In general, the owner's policy covers the immediate family and any other driver who has permission to use the vehicle. The limit of liability that is shown in the policy is the maximum limit for all damages that may result from any one accident, regardless of the number of vehicles or people involved in the accident.

(2) **Medical payments.**

This covers medical costs for the driver and passengers, if the driver is at fault. Generally, this coverage is mandatory in Canada.

(3) **Collision coverage.**

The importance of physical damage coverage to a vehicle is directly proportional to the value of the vehicle, and to the owner's ability to replace or repair the damage. Collision coverage pays for damage sustained in an accident for which the vehicle owner is at fault. Any damage suffered in a collision for which the other driver is at fault is covered by the other driver's automobile policy, under the property damage coverage.

(4) **Comprehensive coverage.**

Comprehensive coverage is a form of "all risks" automobile physical damage coverage. Comprehensive policies pay for damage, resulting from non-accident causes such as a theft, fire, and vandalism. In order to be covered the damage must be from accidental rather than intentional means. For example, if someone locks their keys in the car and then breaks the window in order to retrieve the key's, this is considered intentional and is not covered.

(5) **Uninsured or under insured motorists coverage.**

This is mandatory coverage. This provision covers bodily injury caused by another driver who is uninsured or under insured. This provision also protects against injuries suffered in a hit and run accident.

Insurance policy evaluation checklists

Life insurance policy evaluation

- Is the policy permanent or term coverage?
- Is the beneficiary designation current?
- What is the credit rating of the issuing insurance company?
- What is the purpose of the policy?
- When was the last time an insurance needs analysis was performed?
- What are the settlement options provided by the policy?
- What are the non-forfeiture options?
- What interest rate is charged on policy loans?
- What riders are included with the policy?
- Are the chosen riders still relevant?
- Which dividend option has been chosen?
- Which investment option has been chosen for a UL policy?

Disability insurance policy evaluation

- Is the policy noncancellable and guaranteed renewable?
- Is the definition of disability appropriate for the individual?
- How long is the elimination period?
- What is the insurers credit rating?
- For how long are benefits payable?
- What is the amount of the benefits payable?
- Is a partial disability covered?
- Does the policy cover residual disabilities?
- Are there any riders included with the policy?

Homeowners insurance policy evaluation

- Is the policy based on actual cost or replacement value?
- Is the amount of coverage appropriate?

- Is there personal property that needs to be listed and insured separately?
- Are covered buildings insured for at least 80% of the replacement value?
- Is the amount of liability coverage appropriate?
- Is the policy "specified perils" or "all risks"?

Automobile insurance

- How much are the deductibles?
- Is collision coverage necessary on an older vehicle?
- Is there coverage for uninsured motorists?
- Is the amount of liability coverage adequate?

Glossary

Accidental death benefit. The rider added to a life insurance policy that provides for the payment of an additional benefit if death occurs by accidental means. Often referred to as "double indemnity".

Acquisition cost. The costs of administration, sales commission, and underwriting which are included when issuing a new insurance policy.

Adhesion contract. A standard contract prepared by the insurer. These contracts allow no opportunity to negotiate the terms within the contract.

Adverse selection. The inclination or propensity for poor insurance risks to seek new or continued insurance coverage, which is to their financial benefit, and is to the detriment of the insurance underwriter and/or carrier.

Age limits. The minimum and/or maximum age limits for which an insurer will issue or renew an insurance policy.

Aggregate indemnity. The maximum dollar limit for which a claim may be paid, under an existing insurance policy.

Aleatory contract. A contract in which the benefits or losses sustained depends upon unpredictable, or uncertain conditions.

All risk or all peril. A form of property and casualty insurance which covers against any loss except those which are specifically excluded within the policy contract.

Annual renewable term insurance (ART). Life insurance usually found in group insurance contracts. The premium rate is recalculated every year based on attained age and therefore, higher mortality rate.

Application. A written form supplied by and then returned to the insurance company. It details the type and amount of insurance required, payment method, and other data that enable the underwriter to evaluate the risk and to determine the necessary premium.

Assignment. The method by which an interest in an insurance policy is transferred from one party to another. This usually occurs when a permanent life insurance policy is used as collateral for a loan.

Attained age or insurance age. A person's age, on a specific date.

Beneficiary. The party named to receive the proceeds or other rights of an insurance policy. The beneficiary may be a person or corporation.

Binder. A written notification whereby the insurance company agrees to insure another party while awaiting receipt and underwriting of the application.

Blanket coverage. A policy for which the stated face amount applies to all coverage's.

Broker. An individual who solicits and places insurance business with a variety of insurance companies. Represents the buyer of insurance rather than the insurance company.

Canadian Life and Health Insurance Compensation Corporation (CompCorp). The principal objective of CompCorp is to protect, within limits, Canadian policyholders against loss of benefits. The protection limits per individual are $200,000 of life insurance, $60,000 of savings, with separate limits for registered and non-registered savings, $60,000 limits for each of group savings or individuals savings, and $2,000 per month for retirement or disability annuity benefits. Health insurance benefits are also insured to a separate $60,000 limit. CompCorp meets its commitments through assessments of its member companies.

Carrier. Commercial insurance company that underwrites and administers various insurance services.

Cash surrender value (CSV). The net proceeds that are available from the termination of a whole life insurance policy. The CSV is a percentage of the policy's reserve.

Certificate. Document that is provided to group insurance plan members which outlines coverage and other specific details.

Co-insurance. That proportion or share of an insurance claim which must be paid by the insured.

Contingent beneficiary. The party who will be benefited in case of the death of the primary beneficiary.

Conversion. The contractual privilege granting a party the right to convert an insurance policy to a permanent insurance policy, without evidence of medical insurability.

Creditors group life insurance. Life insurance issued through a lending institution that re-pays debt in case of the borrower's death.

Deductible. The amount of out-of-pocket expense which must be paid by the insured before a claim becomes payable by the insurance carrier.

Disability income insurance. A form of accident and sickness insurance that provides periodic payments, should the insured become unable to work due to illness or accident.

Dismemberment. The loss of a limb, sight, or hearing.

Effective date. The date on which insurance coverage begins. If not stated in the policy, the policy is presumed to take effect at 12:01 a.m. on the effective date.

Elimination period. The length of time between the beginning of a person's disability and the start of a policy's disability benefit.

Endowment insurance. A life insurance policy payable to the insured, if alive, on the policy's maturity date. If the insured is deceased, the policy proceeds are paid to the beneficiary. A policy is said to endow when the cash surrender value is equal to the death benefit of the policy.

Endorsement. A rider that modifies a property and casualty insurance policy.

Evidence of insurability. Proof of an individual's health status, occupation, or any other factors that affect approval for insurance coverage.

Exclusions. Specific instances or occurrences listed in the policy, for which insurance coverage is not provided.

Face amount or face value. The amount payable to the beneficiary upon the death of the insured.

Family income policy. Life insurance policy that pays death benefits monthly rather than as a lump sum.

Grace period. The specified time, after which a premium is due, that an insurance policy's protection will remain in force.

Group insurance. Any insurance plan under which individuals with some common interest such as a union, association, or group of employees and their dependents are insured under a single contract or policy. Most commonly provided types of group insurance are life, disability, and health coverage.

Guaranteed insurability or guaranteed issue underwriting. A rider, available on a life insurance policy, which provides for the purchase of additional insurance at various specified future times without the requirement of medical evidence.

Guaranteed renewable contract. An insurance contract wherein the insured has the right to continue the coverage upon payment of premium, until some pre-specified future date. The insurance carrier cannot alter the contract while it is in force.

Health insurance. Insurance protection that provides payment for covered sickness or injury.

Hospital benefits. An insurance policy that provides coverage for hospital charges. These plans may cover all or part of the actual hospital expense incurred by the insured.

Incontestable clause. A life insurance policy clause that makes the policy indisputable after a specified time period (usually 2 years) has elapsed. Allows the insurance company to void the policy, for specific reasons, during the first 2 years.

Indemnity. A legal concept which limits the recovery under an insurance policy to the lesser of the actual cash value of the loss and the amount which will restore the insured to the pre-loss condition.

Insurable interest. The financial and/or emotional stake of a party in the life of another individual. Life insurance policies with no insurable interest are not enforceable, unless a written permission is obtained from the life insured.

Insurability. All of the factors for an individual such as health, life expectancy, and occupational risk which influence the ability to obtain insurance coverage.

Irrevocable beneficiary. A life insurance policy beneficiary whose interest in the policy cannot be changed without the written permission of the beneficiary.

Joint life policy. A single life insurance policy that covers 2 or more lives. The policy may provide for payment of benefit after the first death (joint and first to die) or alternatively, the policy may provide for payment after the death of the second party (joint and second to die). These types of policies are often used for estate planning purposes.

Key employee or key person insurance. A means of protecting a corporation or business against the financial loss caused by the death of a key individual.

Lapse. Termination of an insurance policy for failure to pay premiums.

Life expectancy. The statistical average number of years, based on mortality tables, that a person of a given age is expected to live.

Loading charge. The amount added to the pure cost of insurance. This load includes amounts used for administration, sales commission, taxes, contingency reserves, and profits.

Medical Information Bureau (MIB). An organization that maintains the insurability records of individuals who have applied for life insurance.

Morbidity. A term used in disability insurance. A morbidity table indicates the incidence of sickness in a large group of individuals.

Mortality. A term used in life insurance. A mortality table indicates the number of deaths in a large group of individuals.

Noncancellable and guaranteed renewable policy. Insurance policy in which the insured has the right to continue coverage until a specified future date, by the payment of premiums when they are due. The insurer cannot make changes to the insurance policy while it is in force.

Non-forfeiture options or provisions. All whole life policies have non-forfeiture provisions. These contractual privileges provide the policyholder with options to maintain the policy in force.

Non-occupational policy. A disability insurance policy that insures an individual against accident and sickness while off the job.

Ordinary life or straight life. Alternative names given to whole life policies.

Paid-up. Policies, on which no further premiums are to be made; however, the insurer is liable for the benefits provided under the terms in the contract.

Participating insurance. Life insurance policy on which the owner receives policy dividends which reflect the difference between the premium charged and the actual experience and surplus earnings or profit of the insurance company.

Policy. The written contract between the insurance company and the policyowner.

Policy reserves. The specific amount allocated, and which is legally required by the insurance company to pay the policy's obligation.

Policy term. The time frame for which an insurance policy provides coverage.

Pre-existing condition. A verifiable medical condition (physical or mental) that existed prior to the issue of the insurance policy. Under some policies, pre-existing conditions are excluded from coverage.

Premium. The term used for the rate charged for a given insurance policy or annuity contract. The amount payable to the company for the benefits provided under a specific contract.

Rated policy. An insurance policy which is issued to a substandard risk. A rated policy may carry a higher premium than a standard policy, or the policy may be issued with specific limitations and exclusions.

Reinstatement. The re-commencement of a lapsed insurance policy. In order to be reinstated the insured must comply with conditions which are specified in the policy, such as paying all outstanding premiums and submitting proof of insurability.

Reinsurance. In order to limit its maximum loss on any one insurance policy, an insurance company often lays off or cedes part of the risk to other insurance companies.

Renewal. The continuation of coverage under a policy beyond its original term by re-establishing the contract for a new term. This is accomplished by accepting the premium for the new term.

Replacement. The procedure for terminating an existing contract of insurance with a new insurance contract. Provincial insurance legislation typically requires the replacing agent or broker to file disclosure paperwork with the company that issued the original contract.

Rider or endorsement. An amendment of the standard policy contract. These modifications change the benefits in exchange for an increased premium.

Segregated fund. A separate and distinct fund maintained by an insurer from which the benefits of an individual variable insurance contract are provided.

Single premium. The lump sum required to cover the entire cost of a life insurance or annuity contract. Calculated as the discounted present value of all future cash flows.

Standard risk. An individual who is considered by the insurance company to have an average likelihood of loss.

Subrogation. The substitution of one party for another when claiming a right or debt.

Substandard risk or impaired risk. An individual considered by the insurance company to have a greater than average likelihood of loss.

Term insurance. Life insurance that is paid to a beneficiary only if the insured dies within a specified period or term. If the life insured survives, the policy expires worthlessly.

Total disability. An accident, illness or injury that prevents an individual from continuously performing each and every duty required of their occupation. **Definitions vary among insurance policies.**

TRAC. TRAC is a Canadian company, which publishes an annual evaluation of all life insurance companies licensed in Canada. Individuals can order detailed financial reports of an insurance company from TRAC.

Underwrite. To insure. The process includes identifying and classifying the risks to which an applicant is exposed.

Unilateral contract. The unilateral contract is an agreement in which only one party makes an enforceable promise. Insurance policies are unilateral contracts since the insured can stop premium payment at anytime however the insurer cannot revoke coverage unless the insured fails to pay the premium.

Universal Life (UL). An interest sensitive form of term life insurance, with flexible premiums, offering tax-deferred cash values.

Variable life. An interest sensitive form of life insurance with flexible premiums offering variable cash values. The premiums vary depending upon the performance of the underlying market index.

Waiver. A document that exempts from coverage certain events or circumstances which are normally covered or required by the policy.

Workers compensation. Benefits and conditions which are set by provincial law, providing payments and/or medical care to an employee for injuries or disease which are sustained or contracted in the course, or the performance of, their employment.

Yearly renewable term (YRT). Life insurance usually found in group insurance contracts. The premium rate is recalculated every year based on attained age and therefore, higher mortality rate.

Questions

1) An individual already has life insurance coverage. How do they determine if and when additional life insurance coverage is required?

The requirement for life insurance coverage will vary from situation to situation and typically depends upon an individual's age, their stage in the life cycle, and their familial obligations. There are a number of methods that can be used to determine an individual's life insurance requirements. These methods range from the general and very simple rules of thumb to more sophisticated and individualized calculations. The most accurate method of determining the required life insurance coverage at any age is the use of a life insurance needs analysis.

2) If a homeowner has lender (mortgagee) provided mortgage life insurance, what happens to this insurance after the mortgage is paid out?

Mortgage insurance is designed to cover the mortgagor (the borrower) over the life of the mortgage and it will cease upon mortgage payout.

3) Disability insurance is expensive. An individual believes that the cost is not affordable.

Disability insurance premiums are expensive compared to life insurance policy premiums. The reason is that the probability of an individual (under retirement age) becoming disabled is much higher than the probability that the same individual will die. Generally this statement is true for the population up until approximately retirement age, at which point the probability of death becomes higher than the probability of a disability.

Actuaries calculate that the probability, in any given year, is that:

- 1 in 106 people die,
- 1 in 88 homes catch fire,
- 1 in 70 vehicles are involved in an accident,

- 1 in 8 people become disabled.

Since the pure cost of any insurance policy is a function of the probability of an occurrence, the number of individuals sharing or pooling the risk, and the cost of the compensation paid, one would expect a disability insurance policy to have higher premiums than a life insurance policy. In this case, based upon the statistics given above one should not be surprised to learn that disability policy insurance premiums are significantly more costly than life insurance policy premiums.

4) What is a life insurance needs analysis?

Not every individual requires life insurance coverage. However, everyone should evaluate their situation and quantify their need for life insurance. This can be accomplished by performing a life insurance needs analysis.

A life insurance needs analysis approximates the amount of life insurance that is required in order to provide a specified level of income following the death of the insured. The life-insurance needs analysis should be done for each of the spouses. The death of a non-working spouse can cause hardship and often requires an increase in domestic expenses.

There are numerous methods for estimating life-insurance requirements. The 2 most common are the expense method and the income method.

The expense method.

The most commonly used method of estimating life-insurance needs is the expense method. The expense method attempts to calculate the present value (PV) of the survivors future expenses in order to maintain current lifestyle.

This method starts with the estimation of the family's lump sum requirements for cash at the time of death. Cash is usually required for expenses such as burial, medical expenses, income taxes, probate fees and capital gains taxes. There may also be a requirement for funds to educate children, to repay a mortgage or other uninsured loans such as credit cards or an automobile loan.

The next step is to calculate the ongoing income of the family. Income sources may include the CPP survivors pensions, CPP orphans pensions, investment income, and earning power of the surviving spouse. The difference between the funds required to meet the family's income needs and the ongoing family income, is the face amount of life insurance required.

The income method.

The income method attempts to estimate the life-insurance requirements by calculating the present value (PV) of an individual's future income stream. The difficulties in using the income method revolve around attempting to determine the discount rate at which to compute the PV and estimating the growth rate of the individual's future earnings stream.

5) How can a retiree ensure that long-term care coverage remains in force, should an individual's health or spouse's health change?

Long-term care coverage is now available from some insurance companies in Canada. Long-term care policies are designed to provide funds when an individual can no longer care for themselves and requires either specialized nursing care, or institutionalization. These policies can be established as stand-alone policies or may be available as a rider on a life insurance policy.

6) A self-employed business owner has no insurance coverage of any type. How can this individual prioritize the insurance coverage that may be required?

An individual should first identify and analyze the risks that they are faced with. After identifying the risks, the individual should evaluate the severity of the potential loss from each of the risks. Would the loss be critical, from a financial perspective, or would it merely be inconvenient? The next step is to determine how frequently the individual is exposed to each of these perils or dangers.

Once the individual business owner has determined the nature and the frequency of the risks, it can then be determined which of the four methods (retention, avoidance, reduction, or transfer) of managing risk can best be employed for each of the hazards.

7) A homeowner has just taken out a new mortgage and the financial institution offered life insurance coverage. Should the homeowner accept this coverage?

Typically, this type of creditors group insurance can only be purchased when initially applying for the financing, it cannot usually be added later. Since this coverage is relatively easy to qualify for, from a medical underwriting perspective, there can be little harm in accepting the offer. This strategy would be advisable to a consumer who has not previously investigated their life-insurance situation. The danger to declining the creditors coverage, occurs when the individual finds that they are unable to obtain their required life-insurance coverage elsewhere for any one of a number of reasons.

If the individual obtains the appropriate life-insurance coverage elsewhere, they can terminate the group creditor coverage at their leisure.

8) How does an individual determine the correct amount of vehicle liability insurance required?

A third party claim against a driver could reduce or eliminate their net worth very quickly. Therefore, most financial advisors recommend that a minimum of $1 million of third party liability coverage be purchased. Additionally, if driving in a foreign country particularly the USA, one would be well advised to purchase additional liability insurance in order to protect, in the rare event, that the driver is found liable to others.

9) Does the government provide Canadians with any insurance protection?

Canada Pension Plan (CPP).

In addition to retirement benefits the Canada Pension Plan provides disability benefits to contributors who become disabled. Since January 1, 1998, in order to collect a disability pension, CPP contributors must be between 18 and 65 years of age and must have contributed to CPP in four of the last six years. Additionally, in order to collect CPP disability benefits it must be medically determined that an individual is so severely disabled as to be unable to perform any substantially gainful employment. Any disability, whether caused by physical or mental means would be considered, providing it was of a long-term and persistent nature.

The monthly disability pension is composed of 2 parts; a flat rate, plus 75% of the contributor's retirement pension. As at January 1, 1999, the flat rate portion is $339.80. The maximum monthly pension payable is $903.55. Although it is possible to collect benefits retroactively, the contributor is restricted to a maximum of 12 months of retroactive payments. Disability payments cease when the recipient recovers, dies, or reaches age 65 and / or starts to receive a CPP retirement pension.

Moreover, if the disabled individual contributor has children under the age of 18, or under the age of 25 if they are in full-time attendance at school or university, each child is eligible to receive a monthly pension of $171.33.

CPP provides protection in case of the death of the contributor who has paid into CPP for a specified length of time. CPP provides a lump sum death benefit of up to six times the monthly retirement pension to a maximum of $2,500. CPP also provides a pension to a qualifying surviving spouse and to dependent children. As of January 1, 1999, a surviving spouse between the ages of 45 and 64 would receive a pension composed of a flat rate ($132.58) plus 37.5% of the deceased contributor's retirement pension to a maximum on $414.46 per month. A surviving spouse under the age of 45 is entitled to a reduced pension.

For each month that the survivor was under the age of 45, at the time of the contributor's death, the pension is reduced by 1/120. If a surviving spouse is under age 45 and is disabled or has dependent children, they are entitled to receive an unreduced pension.

If the surviving spouse is under age 35, is not disabled, and has no dependent children, then no pension amounts are payable.

Surviving spouses over the age 65 can receive a maximum survivors pension of $414.46 per month, at the time of writing. Survivors pensions are payable for life and do not cease upon remarriage.

The orphans pension is payable to dependent children under the age of 18, or 25 if they are in full-time attendance at school. The orphans pension is currently $171.33 per month.

It is important to remember that CPP benefits are taxable.

Workers Compensation (WCB).

Workers Compensation is a provincially regulated insurance plan for occupational accident and sickness. The premiums charged for Workers Compensation are paid by the employer. The Workers Compensation plans cover many workers in most industries, although there are exemptions or exceptions for example, self-employed individuals. A covered disability must arise while on the job, and be work-related. Workers Compensation would not normally cover an individual while travelling to or from work.

Workers Compensation benefits vary from province to province, but monetary benefits are tax-free. Typically, any payments or benefits received under an employer provided disability plan or private disability insurance policy are integrated and will be reduced by any amounts that are received from Workers Compensation. In other words, Workers Compensation is considered first payer.

Employment Insurance (EI).

In addition to providing benefits to unemployed individuals, EI pays for up to 15 weeks of sickness benefits and maternity benefits, and up to 10 weeks of parental benefits. There is usually a 2-week waiting period before benefits start and any benefits received are taxable. The maximum benefits available are currently $413.00 per week.

10) How are the dividends paid on a participating life insurance policy taxed?

The dividends received by a participating policyholder are technically a refund of premium paid. Therefore, the dividends paid on a participating life insurance policy are received on a tax-free basis. However, if the dividends are left with the insurance company to accumulate and earn interest or are otherwise left to invest with the insurance company, the investment income is taxable annually.

CHAPTER 4

Canadian Retirement Accumulation Programs

Pension benefits and pension legislation in Canada are continually evolving. An understanding of the pension benefits an individual may be entitled to upon retirement is necessary in order to realistically plan retirement savings and postretirement cash flows.

1) Government pensions

A) Old Age Security (OAS)

The *Old Age Security Act* was enacted in 1952 and replaced prior provincially mandated legislation established in the 1920s. Several improvements were introduced thereafter. In 1965, the age for eligibility of the OAS pension benefit was reduced to age 65 from age 70. The introduction of cost of living indexation occurred in 1972 and in 1973, OAS payments became indexed quarterly to the consumer price index (CPI). Legislation introduced in 1977 allowed for the payment of a partial pension.

OAS has been further improved through the 1980s and 1990s to better aid low-income widows and widowers. OAS is payable to most Canadians who reach age 65 and is funded through general tax revenues. OAS is not automatic; it must be applied for, and does not depend upon an individual being retired. OAS benefits can be applied for up to one year in advance of the annuitant's 65th birthday.

The pension benefit received may be either a full or a partial pension depending upon the number of years that an annuitant resides in Canada after the age of 18. A full pension is payable to a person who has resided in Canada for 40 years or more after the age of 18.

A partial pension is payable to a person who has resided in Canada for at least 10 years after reaching the age 18. Providing that an annuitant had resided in Canada for at least 20 years after reaching 18 years of age, the OAS pension may be paid to individuals who currently reside outside of Canada.

Current maximum OAS pension benefits are approximately $411.23 per month at the time of writing. For income tax purposes, OAS benefits are considered taxable income, when the benefits are received. Additionally, since 1989, OAS benefits have been subject to a claw back. Approximately 15% of the OAS pension is clawed back at an income level of $53,000. OAS is fully clawed back (i.e. 100%) at an income level of approximately $84,500.

B) Canada Pension Plan (CPP)

The Canada Pension Plan (CPP) was enacted in 1965 and applies to almost everyone, over the age of 18, who has been employed in Canada. CPP is a contributory and earnings related pension and insurance program. Since 1965, legislation has been passed a number of times to improve the CPP benefits. These improvements include:

- the exclusion of low income earning periods,
- the ability to share or divide pension credits between spouses,
- the continuation of survivor's benefits to a spouse who remarries, and
- the inclusion of a common law spouse's ability to share CPP pensions.

In 1998, the CPP system moved from a pay as you go financing mechanism to a more complete and fuller funding, which entails increases in the contribution rate and the introduction of the new CPP investment policy.

The CPP investment board, which consists of qualified professionals, is independent of provincial and federal governments and is mandated to follow the same general investment rules that govern other types of pension plans. The investment board will report its investment results to the Canadian public on a regular and ongoing basis. At the time of writing, CPP funds have been used or invested in provincial bonds that have provided the provinces with a low-cost (subsidized) source of funds. With the creation of the CPP investment board, some changes in the ability of the provinces to fund borrowing through the issue of provincial bonds will result. These provincial bonds must now carry the same interest rate as the provinces pay on their other loans, rather than the lower interest rates the provinces have thus far been enjoying.

CPP provides three types of benefits:

(1) Disability benefits to the contributor, including benefits payable to a disabled annuitant's children to the age of 18,

(2) Survivor's benefits that include a lump sum death benefit and pensions to a surviving spouse and their children, and a

(3) Retirement pension.

Unlike OAS, which is funded from general tax revenues, CPP is a contributory program.

Since CPP is a contributory program that depends upon employment, the ability to participate in CPP is subject to qualifying income levels. In order to participate, an annuitant must earn a certain minimum income. The minimum income is specified as the yearly basic earnings (YBE) and is currently approximately $3,500 per annum. CPP is also subject to a maximum cap or ceiling level of earnings, which is known as the yearly maximum pensionable earnings (YMPE). The YMPE is adjusted at the beginning of every year and is currently approximately $36,900 per annum. The difference between the 2 numbers, which is called pensionable earnings, is therefore, $33,400. Both employees and employers contribute to CPP. Currently each contributes 3.2% of the employee's contributable earnings. A self-employed individual contributes 6.4% of their pensionable earnings.

The normal retirement age for CPP benefits is 65. Currently the maximum retirement pension payable by CPP is $750 per month. However, retirement benefits can begin as early as age 60 or benefits can be delayed until as late as age 70. If an annuitant continues to work, contributions can be made into the CPP program until age 70.

A retiree who begins to receive CPP benefits before the normal retirement age of 65 receives a reduced pension and conversely, a retiree who delays receipt of CPP benefits, until after age 65, receives an enhanced pension.

The reduction in retirement benefits is equal to 0.5% per month for each month that benefits are paid before the annuitant reaches age 65. In other words, the retiree who decides to receive CPP benefits beginning at age 60 will receive a pension that is reduced by 30% from the normal retirement pension. This is calculated as 0.5% per month times 60 months which equals a 30% reduction in retirement pension benefits.

A retiree who delays receipt of CPP pension benefits until age 70 will receive an enhancement in their pension of 0.5% per month for 60 months or 30%.

2) Employer-sponsored registered pension plans (RPP)

A registered pension plan (RPP) is an employer-sponsored retirement savings scheme that is designed with the intention to reward long term and loyal service to an employer with a lifetime of income. Registered plans are administered by a trustee, and must comply with certain conditions imposed by Revenue Canada and provincial government pension standards. RPPs qualify for tax advantages on the part of the employer and employee. The funds accumulated within a registered pension plan are protected from the annuitant's creditors.

An employer's determination to establish an RPP is a major decision, which is not undertaken without planning and deliberation. There are contractual obligations on the part of the employer once the decision to implement an RPP has been taken.

An employer must contribute specified amounts to an RPP that is set up for the benefit of the employees according to the pension plan's contractual requirements.

Normal retirement age in a pension plan is most often set at age 65. If an employee decides to retire before age 65, there is usually a reduction in the retirement pension. Most RPPs allow for retirement as early as age 55.

An RPP is said to be either contributory or non-contributory. In the case of a contributory RPP, the employee is required to contribute to the pension plan in addition to the contributions made on the employee's behalf by the employer. Conversely, a non-contributory pension plan requires no contribution on the part of the employee; the employer alone funds all contributions. In any event, the employer must provide at least 50% of the annual pension benefit earned.

Once an RPP has vested, the employee gains certain rights over all of the monies within the pension plan, irrespective of who originally contributed the funds to the RPP. The length of time required before vesting occurs varies from province to province but as a rule, vesting takes place after 2 years of employment. These rights can be exercised when an employee terminates his/her employment, whether by dismissal or resignation. Since the intent of an RPP is to provide a lifetime of income there are, by necessity, certain restrictions placed on the options available to an employee with respect to these vested pension monies. Unless the funds are of a minimal amount, they cannot be taken out as a lump sum of cash.

Pension benefit standards legislation allows the following termination options for vested RPP funds:

(1) The funds may be left with the plan, where they will continue to grow, although no new contributions will be made to the plan,

(2) The funds may be transferred to a new pension plan, providing the new plan allows such transfers,

(3) The funds may be transferred to a "locked in" registered retirement savings plan (RRSP), or

(4) The funds may be transferred to a locked in retirement arrangement (LIRA).

A locked in RRSP in no way restricts the annuitant's ability to invest the funds. Any investment, which qualifies to be held within an RRSP, will also qualify to be held within a locked in RRSP. The lock in provision, however, does restrict the ability of the annuitant to gain access to the funds. The lock in provision **does not allow**, at this time, an annuitant to gain access to the funds within a locked in RRSP using a RRIF. The province in which the pension plan is domiciled will determine the options available to the annuitant for the maturation of their locked in funds. For example, currently in BC, locked in RRSPs can only be matured using a type of life annuity or a life income fund (LIF). The lock in provision will also restrict or specify a minimum age (usually age 55) at which time the funds within the locked in RRSP can be accessed.

The annuitant cannot access funds from a locked-in RRSP as a lump sum cash withdrawal. The money has to stay in the locked in RRSP, and must be used to buy a life annuity at retirement age. However, under the pension laws of certain provinces, pension funds or funds from a locked-in RRSP can be transferred to a **locked-in RRIF**. These locked-in RRIFs are known as locked-in retirement income funds (LRIFs).

If an employee dies before retirement, the pension plan documents will detail the benefits available to the surviving spouse or to the estate. Provincial legislation dictates the minimum death benefits that an RPP must provide.

There are 2 basic types of registered pension plans:

(i) Defined benefit plans, and

(ii) Defined contribution or money purchase plans

i) Defined benefit plans

As the name suggests, a defined benefit pension plan pays a pension to the annuitant that is based on a defined formula. The formula is normally some combination of years of pensionable service and a percentage of earnings. Under the terms of the defined benefit pension plan an actuary can estimate the pension benefit that will be received by an annuitant based upon certain actuarial assumptions, including an employee's current salary, future wage increases and investment returns earned on pension plan assets. For example, a defined benefit plan may pay an annuitant 2% of earnings for each of 35 years of pensionable service; this would entitle the annuitant to 70% of their pre-retirement earnings. The 2% of earnings formula is the richest plan that is allowed by Revenue Canada.

There are a number of methods that are used when determining a defined benefit plan's pension payment:

(1) The defined benefit plan may pay a flat benefit.

Although this formula is not common, it is found in some unionized collective agreements. In terms of this type of plan, the annuitant may be entitled to some flat amount of pension such as $50 per month for each year of service provided to the employer. For example, an employee with 25 years service using the previous example, would be entitled to pension of $50 per month per year times 25 years = $1250 per month.

(2) The formula may be based upon a career average of earnings.

This is simply the arithmetic average of the annuitant's annual salary. Consider an employee who spends 35 years with an employer. This employee may have started a career earning $5,000 per annum and is now earning $150,000. This employee's average salary over their career may, for example, be $65,000. Based upon 35 years of service and 2% of average earnings the annuitant would be entitled to a pension of 35 times 2% times $65,000, which equals an annual pension of $45,500.

(3) The formula may be based upon the annuitant's final average of earnings.

For example, the average of the last 5 years earnings. Continuing the example from above in which the employee has final earnings of $150,000, they may have average final earnings of $125,000. This is a dramatic difference from the career average earnings in the example above!

Caution! An overall restriction exists which limits the maximum pension payable under a defined benefit plan to $1,722 times the number of years of pensionable service. Therefore, continuing the example, the annuitant described in situation #3 above would be limited or restricted to a maximum pension of $1,722 times 35 years of service or $60,270 per annum. Where $1,722 is the maximum annual earned benefit entitlement that is currently allowed under pension benefit standards.

With the defined benefit plan, an employer is contracting i.e. promising to pay a specified pension at retirement to an employee. Therefore, if through poor investment performance there are insufficient funds at retirement to fully fund an employee's pension, the employer must make good on the promised pension and the employer must, in some manner, acquire these monies usually from continuing operations. In other words, under the terms of the defined benefit pension plan the employer shoulders all of the investment risk. In order to minimize the possibility of investment shortfalls defined benefit pension plan assets and liabilities are required to be examined by an actuary at least once every three years (triennially). Furthermore, the actuary calculates and prepares the pension adjustment (PA) statement that is factored into the calculation of the amount that an employee can contribute to an RRSP.

ii) Defined contribution or money purchase pension plans (MPP)

Under the terms of the defined contribution or money purchase pension plan, what is known in advance is not the final pension that the annuitant receives, but the amount that is contributed into the pension plan. This contribution is a specified percentage of earnings. The maximum amount that can be contributed annually into a money purchase plan on behalf of an employee is currently $13,500 or 18% of "earned income". There is no guarantee from the employer regarding the final pension amount that the annuitant is to receive at retirement.

The pension adjustment (PA) is very easy to calculate for a money purchase pension plan. The PA is simply calculated as the sum of the amount that the employer contributes on behalf of the employee plus the employee's contributions.

The services of an actuary are not required with the money purchase pension plan. The employer's responsibility ceases when the contribution is made to the employee's pension plan. There is no further obligation on behalf of the employer. In this respect, a money purchase pension plan is similar to an RRSP in that there is no foreknowledge of the amount of pension to actually be received. The pension received at retirement by an employee is determined by three factors: the total amount accumulated in the pension plan, the interest rate in effect at the time the pension plan is annuitized, and the length of time for which pension benefits are to be received.

Which type of pension plan is best?

The answer to this question depends upon a number of factors.

Over the past decade we have witnessed the downsizing of many corporations and the related cost cutting and re-engineering that have characterized the 1990s. One method of cost saving has been for corporations to move away from providing employees with defined benefit pension plans and instead corporations are providing money purchase pension plans. Cost savings result because money purchase pension plans do not require the services of an actuary, the administration costs are lower with the money purchase plan, and the use of money purchase plans have decreased the employer's investment risk. As explained previously, in defined benefit pension plans if there are unfunded plan liabilities at the time of an employee's retirement the employer must make good on the promised pension. Conversely, with the money purchase pension plan the employee shoulders all of the investment risks in that there is no promise of a specified pension amount and the employer's obligations cease upon contribution to the plan. It is not surprising then, to see the move in the marketplace, towards the increased usage of money purchase plans.

In general terms, a defined benefit pension plan is most valuable to an employee who is in his or her 50s and whose earnings are over $75,000, in other words, a highly compensated individual who has a relatively short time until retirement. The money purchase plan, on the other hand, is most attractive to a younger employee who has a longer time horizon over which to allow the contributions to compound and whose earnings will no doubt rise over time.

Defined benefit pension plans can typically be found in the public sector and they are still used by some large employers. It is not unusual to encounter a situation where the executives of the corporation or enterprise will be members of a defined benefit plan while the other employees are members of a money purchase pension plan. Consider that the maximum contribution to a money purchase plan is $13,500 per annum while the maximum contribution to a defined benefit plan is approximately $15,500 per annum. It is also worth noting that defined benefit pension plans can be arranged to provide for certain enhanced benefits. For example, many defined benefit plans provide pensions which are indexed to inflation and which provide augmented death benefits or survivors benefits. However, it is important to note that these enhancements cost more to provide.

Maturity options for registered pension plans

Retirement benefits paid from an RPP are paid in the form of an annuity for the individual's lifetime. There are a number of basic options, which include:

(1) **Life only annuity.**

Under this option, funds accumulated in the pension plan are used to purchase an income or pension that continues for as long as the annuitant is alive. This option is also known as a straight life, or ordinary life annuity. The advantage of the straight life annuity is that it pays the highest available monthly pension. The disadvantage of the life annuity is that when the annuitant dies all payments cease. This option would be attractive to an unmarried annuitant, or to an annuitant that has neither family obligations nor a desire to provide benefits after death.

For example, assume for the purposes of discussion that an annuitant has accumulated sufficient funds, and that interest rates are such that these funds are enough to provide a life annuity of $2,000 per month. This would be the straight life annuity payment to the annuitant.

(2) **Joint and last survivor annuity.**

Under this type of annuity option, benefits are payable not only for the life of the annuitant but will continue after the annuitant's death to the surviving spouse for as long as the surviving spouse is alive. This is a more attractive option to an annuitant that has a spouse and wishes to provide income for the spouse's remaining lifetime. Under pension benefit standards a joint and last survivor annuity option is the standard provision required under legislation. In order to waive this option both spouses will be required to sign waiver disclaimers. This requirement is in place in order to protect the rights of the spouse and prevents the annuitant from unilaterally disinheriting the spouse. When determining the pension to be provided to both the annuitant and the surviving spouse an actuary will consider the amount of retirement funds accumulated, current interest rates, and the life expectancies of both the annuitant and spouse. It is typical for a surviving spouse to receive a pension that is reduced after the death of the annuitant. It is not uncommon for the surviving spouse's pension to be 60% of the pension that was received while the annuitant was alive. It may be possible to arrange the annuity in such a manner that there is no reduction upon the death of the annuitant, in which case, a lower pension would be payable during both lifetimes.

Using the previous assumption of the straight life annuity of $2,000, in the case of the joint survivor option the annuitant might receive a lifetime pension of $1,600 per month and after the annuitant's death, the surviving spouse would receive 60% or $960 per month for their remaining lifetime. Conversely, if it was arranged so that there was no reduction to the surviving spouse upon the death of the annuitant, the pension might be $1,200 per month for the lifetime of both spouses.

It is important to note that since the life expectancy's of both spouses are considered, the difference in ages between the 2 spouses is a major factor determining the pension amounts. Everything else being equal, the larger the spread in ages between spouses the lower the payouts will be. Additionally, once this decision to opt for a joint and survivor pension is taken, it is irrevocable. Note also, that should the annuitant out live the spouse and subsequently remarry, the new spouse has no rights to any part of the survivors pension.

(3) **Life annuity with a guarantee period.** (also called a refund annuity)

Under this annuity option, a specified amount is paid for the annuitant's lifetime. However, in order to protect the surviving spouse there is a guarantee as to the minimum amount repaid to the survivor.

Continuing the example from above, assume a guarantee of 15 years. The annuitant might receive a pension of $1,800 per month for life. Now, suppose that the annuitant dies after receiving 5 years of payments, in which case the surviving spouse would continue to receive $1,800 per month for 10 more years at which time payments cease. Conversely, if the annuitant lives to be 100 years old, the $1,800 per month would continue until the annuitant's death. The annuitant can not out live the pension income since it is a form of a life annuity.

In all of the above examples, the amounts illustrated are fictional, however it should be noted that although the amounts are fictional the relationships between the amounts paid by the different types of life annuity are valid and serve to illustrate the relative costs and benefits of each choice. In other words, it is not unusual in the marketplace, for a life only annuity to pay approximately 20% more than the joint survivor annuity or approximately 10% more than a life annuity with a guarantee. These relationships, of course, will vary with interest rates in the general economy. Anytime that retirement planning is being performed, it is necessary to carefully review the options that can be provided by the specific pension plan in question. These projections should be obtained from the plan itself in the case of a defined benefit plan or the appropriate life annuity pension amounts can be estimated very closely by obtaining quotations from a reputable annuity brokerage firm.

(4) **Life income fund (LIF).**

Under this option pension funds are rolled into the LIF which is somewhat similar to a registered retirement income fund (RRIF), in that a certain minimum and specified income must be paid on an annual basis, but the annuitant may be paid up to a stipulated maximum amount. Unlike a RRIF however, the maximum amount that can be paid by the LIF is restricted. This restriction is a protective feature, which ensures that the annuitant cannot remove all the funds. This restriction is in place because a LIF merely defers, until age 80 (as a maximum), the conversion of the remaining funds into one of the three RPP annuity options previously mentioned. In other words, a LIF merely defers the conversion to an annuity; it does not replace it. Some provinces have introduced a locked in retirement income fund (LRIF) which allows the annuitant to have access to the funds in a manner similar to a RRIF. Over time, more of the provinces will probably move in a similar direction.

3) Deferred profit-sharing plan (DPSP)

A deferred profit-sharing plan (DPSP) is a formally registered savings arrangement whereby an employer contributes a stated percentage of net profits. A DPSP is not subject to any provincial pension legislation. There is usually a clause in the plan that specifies the procedure to be followed in a year of zero profits or losses. Only the employer makes contributions to an employee's DPSP; the employee does not contribute on their own behalf. The maximum allowable annual contribution to a DPSP is $6,750 or 18% of earnings.

The pension adjustment (PA) is easily calculated for a DPSP, it is simply the amount contributed by the employer.

The income from a DPSP is considered, for income tax purposes, to be taxable when received by the employee. The receipt of proceeds from a DPSP would be at normal retirement age or as allowed by the terms of the profit-sharing plan. Unlike registered pension plans, a DPSP may pay lump sum cash payments to an annuitant. The DPSP may also allow transfers to RRSPs, RPPs, or RRIFs.

4) Registered retirement savings plans (RRSP)

Registered retirement savings plans (RRSP) were first introduced into the Canadian marketplace starting in 1957 and have become one the most popular and widely used retirement planning tools available to Canadians.

Most Canadians are familiar with the RRSP's 2 major tax advantages: deduction and deferral.

RRSPs are usually established as a trust. Funds, which are contributed into the trust for the benefit of the beneficiary (the annuitant), by the contributor (settlor), are deductible from income when determining taxable income. Usually the contributor and beneficiary is the same person, however, it is possible for the contributor to designate the spouse as the annuitant. Additionally, any growth that occurs within an RRSP is sheltered from current income taxes until the funds are eventually removed from the shelter of the RRSP. Under current legislation, the RRSP must be matured by the end of the year in which the annuitant turns 69 years of age. At the present time, an RRSP can invest up to 20% of its book value into foreign investments.

Types of RRSPs

There are several types, or classifications, of RRSPs available to Canadians although the *Income Tax Act* treats them identically.

A) Deposit plans.

- Refers to RRSPs that are held with issuers such as banks, trust companies, and credit unions. These plans consist of daily interest savings accounts, certificates of deposit (CDs), term deposits (TDs), and guaranteed investment certificates (GICs). Deposit plans are typically covered by deposit insurance such as Canada Deposit Insurance Corporation (CDIC) or Credit Union Deposit Insurance Corporation (CUDIC) up to specified limits. Deposit plans are generally considered low-risk investments.

B) The Canadian government, through Canada Investment and Savings, has recently introduced Canada Premium Bonds (CPB's).

- CPB's, which were formerly known as Canada RRSP bonds, are available for purchase in RRSPs directly from the Canadian retail debt agency. Previously Canada Savings Bonds (CSBs), although considered qualified RRSP investments, had to be held in a self-directed RRSP.

C) Managed plans.

- Managed plans are offered by numerous financial institutions in Canada including mutual fund companies and insurance companies. These types of plans hold mutual funds, which can be managed either by the issuing institution or by other mutual fund companies. Managed plans may also hold treasury bills and money-market funds.

D) There are certain advantages to owning an RRSP that is issued by a life insurance company.

- These plans are usually considered to be an insurance contract, and under provincial insurance regulations and laws are protected from the claims of creditors in the case of the annuitant's bankruptcy. Unless the funds are held in a locked in RRSP, non-insurance RRSPs are subject to the claims of the annuitant's creditors. This special protection provided to insurance RRSPs could be overruled if it is found by a bankruptcy court that the annuitant transferred funds to the protected insurance RRSP within the last year. If the annuitant was insolvent when the transfer took place, these assets may be seized within the subsequent 5-year period.

E) Self-directed RRSP.

- Self-directed RRSPs are very flexible and offer the individual annuitant full control over, and responsibility for, the investments that are held in the plan. Revenue Canada stipulates that investments held in the self-directed RRSP must be "qualified investments". These qualified investments would include treasury bills (T-bills), CPB's, TDs, GICs, stocks, bonds, mutual funds and mortgages. Holding non-qualifying investments in a self-directed RRSP can attract penalties imposed by Revenue Canada. Self-directed RRSPs, in addition to all of the benefits offered by deposit or managed RRSPs, offer the annuitant additional financial planning opportunities.

RRSP rules

1. **Contribution limits.**

   The maximum amount that an individual can contribute to an RRSP in any given year depends upon the annuitant's previous years income. Revenue Canada currently stipulates that an individual can deduct from income taxes the lesser of $13,500 or 18% of the previous years "earned income" less the annuitant's pension adjustment (PA) for that year. The annuitant's PA is usually reported on the T4 slip, is available from Revenue Canada, and is noted on the annuitant's notice of assessment. A T4 slip is the annual statement produced by employers, which is required to be provided to employees for the purposes of income tax preparation.

"Earned income" is specifically defined within the *Income Tax Act*. According to Revenue Canada's definition, "earned income" includes employment income, net business income, net rental income, and CPP and QPP disability benefits.

If an annuitant does not contribute the maximum RRSP amount that Revenue Canada allows in a given year, these unused deductions are not lost. An annuitant's unused contribution room, from as far back as 1991 may be accumulated and carried forward to future years. In 1996, the rules were altered to allow undeducted amounts to be carried forward indefinitely. These undeducted amounts can be paid into an RRSP anytime in addition to an annuitant's allowable contribution for any year.

Excess contributions can also be made to an RRSP. Since 1995, allowable excess contributions have been limited to a maximum total of $2,000. There are penalties imposed by Revenue Canada upon annuitant's who contribute more than this $2,000 limit. These excess contributions are not tax deductible and violation of the $2,000 limit is subject to penalty taxes of 1% per month, while the excess amounts remain in the RRSP.

2. **Spousal RRSPs.**

Spousal RRSPs allow the annuitant to pre-plan a splitting of income that will benefit both spouses after retirement. The idea is quite simple. The contributor may make deductible contributions within their own normal contribution limits, to an RRSP for his or her spouse. These contributions to the spousal RRSP in no way affect the limits that the spouse may make to his or her own RRSP. Since 1992, the definition of the spouse has included opposite sex common law spouses. As of the time of writing, same-sex spouses are precluded from this planning technique.

Income splitting operates because of the progressive nature of the Canadian income tax system. The progressive nature of the tax system simply means that the more income that is earned, the higher the income tax that is paid. This progressive nature of the Canadian tax system leads to a phenomenon known as the marginal tax rate or tax bracket. Marginal tax rate refers to the amount or rate of tax that is paid on $1 of additional income (at the margin). Income splitting improves after-tax efficiency in that $70,000 of annual income will attract less income taxes if each spouse earns annual income of $35,000, than if one spouse were to pay tax on the entire $70,000.

In order to minimize abuses of this income splitting opportunity, Revenue Canada imposes certain restrictions. The three-year rule states that if the spouse were to withdraw the funds from the spousal RRSP, in the year of withdrawal or the 2 previous tax years, no contributions to a spousal RRSP can be made to any spousal plan. If funds are withdrawn within this three-year period these amounts, up to the amount that was originally deducted, will be attributed back to the contributor spouse and included in their income. The three-year rule does not apply when, at retirement, funds that were contributed to the spousal RRSP are rolled into a RRIF and the minimum income is withdrawn from the RRIF, even if withdrawals begin within the three-year period. However, if more than the minimum amount is withdrawn from the RRIF the three-year rule will apply.

3. **Eligible contributions.**

Although most Canadians contribute cash to an RRSP there is no requirement that the contributions be in this form. Any qualified investment is considered an eligible contribution such as blue-chip stocks or bonds. However, it must be noted that a contribution of eligible qualifying investment is deemed to be a disposition which occurs at current fair market value (FMV) and therefore, any gains realized by this form of transfer will be taxable in the year that the contribution was made. Additionally, any capital losses incurred on such a transfer are not allowable and therefore any asset with accrued losses should usually not be transferred.

Planning with RRSPs

1. **Early contributions.**

Prudent planning dictates that annual contributions be made as early in the year as possible to insure the full benefits of compounding. RRSP contributions for any given tax year must be made within the year or within the first sixty days of the subsequent year. Early contributions may make it possible for the contributor to apply for the reduction of withholding taxes at source as allowed by Revenue Canada.

There is no restriction contained within the *Income Tax Act* that specifies at what minimum age contributions can be made to an RRSP. The Act does, however, stipulate that the annuitant must have "earned income". Other restrictions that exist in the marketplace are likely to have been imposed by a financial institution, not by Revenue Canada. The parents of children who have "earned income" should investigate the feasibility of filing income tax returns on behalf of the child in order to protect or lock in the undeducted RRSP contributions which will benefit the child in later life.

If it is not possible to contribute a lump sum of cash early in the year, an individual should make regular and ongoing contributions to the RRSP. This strategy is referred to as dollar cost averaging. Dollar cost averaging involves setting aside a specific amount of money on a regular basis, usually monthly. The idea is that rather than trying to time an investment decision, which the experts tell us is virtually impossible on a consistent basis, the investor allows the volatility of the markets to work for rather than against him or her. Dollar cost averaging is particularly attractive when investing into volatile vehicles such as equities or when interest rates are moving up and down unpredictably.

This disciplined approach to investing ensures that an investor purchases more when prices are low and purchases less when prices are high. Dollar cost averaging can be viewed as a hedging strategy because of the discipline instilled upon the investor. The more volatile the investment vehicle is, the more beneficial the strategy of dollar cost averaging.

2. **Delayed RRSP deduction.**

The RRSP rules allow a contribution to be made to an RRSP in any particular year, but there is no requirement that the tax deduction be taken in a particular year. This allows the taxpayer the opportunity to take the tax deduction when it is most beneficial. This may be an advantage to someone who has volatile income for example, a commissioned salesperson, who for whatever reason has temporarily low income in one year. The contributed funds will compound on a tax-deferred basis, and an individual will benefit from greater tax saving when income returns to the normal level (higher marginal tax bracket). Delayed deduction may also benefit someone who takes a leave of absence, leaves the workforce temporarily to raise a child, or who becomes a nonresident but will return to Canada at some point in future. The downside to this strategy is that the income tax will be prepaid and therefore one must consider the time value of money when evaluating the appropriateness of this particular strategy.

3. **Spousal RRSPs.**

   As mentioned previously, an individual can make deductible contributions to an RRSP on behalf of a spouse subject to the individual taxpayers overall maximum deductible limit. This strategy can benefit the couple when the spouse is expected to earn less retirement income than the contributor and thereby affect a split of income.

   The use of spousal RRSPs can also be an appropriate strategy when the spouse is younger than the contributor and therefore allows for a longer period of tax deferral. Revenue Canada precludes individuals over the age of 69 from contributing to their own RRSP. However, assuming that the contributor has "earned income", deductible contributions can be made to a spousal RRSP up until the end of the year that the spouse reaches age 69.

4. **RRSP mortgages.**

   It is possible for a taxpayer to arrange a mortgage loan from a self-directed RRSP. This mortgage loan can be used to finance the purchase of a principal residence either for the annuitant or for another non-arms length individual. The rules stipulate that the mortgage must be arranged with the same conditions as those provided by a regular lender. In other words, the interest rate payable on the mortgage loan must be arranged at market rates. The *Income Tax Act* further stipulates that the mortgage must be insured by Canada Mortgage and Housing Corporation (CMHC), and it must be secured by Canadian real estate.

   This strategy is particularly advantageous to an individual whose RRSP is currently invested in GICs, TDs, CPB's, T-bills or other types of deposits. The individual will benefit by any spread that exists between the interest rate paid on any existing mortgage loan and the interest rate earned on the deposits held within the RRSP.

   One must carefully weigh the costs and benefits of this particular strategy. The individual will require a self-directed RRSP for which the annuitant will most likely be charged an annual administration fee. Additionally, there is the added expense of purchasing CMHC insurance, legal fees and any other administrative charges levied by the trustee. Anyone considering this particular strategy must be cognizant of these ongoing fees and expenses; however, it can make a great deal of common sense to employ this strategy and pay interest to oneself rather than to make payments to a financial institution, providing of course, that one has the necessary funds accumulated within the RRSP. This strategy merely reinforces the argument to contribute as early as possible and as much as possible to an RRSP.

5. **Homebuyers' plan. (HBP)**

First time homebuyers may borrow up to $20,000 from their RRSPs in order to finance the purchase of an owner occupied principal residence. An individual is considered a first-time buyer if neither the individual nor their spouse owned their own home and lived in it as their principal residence in any of the 5 calendar years before the withdrawal. If funds are withdrawn from the RRSP to purchase a home, the purchase must be made by October 1 of the year following the withdrawal. These loans must be repaid however, and they can be amortized over periods of up to 15 years, which results in a minimum annual repayment of $1,333. This 15-year repayment period must commence in the second calendar year after withdrawal. If in any year a minimum repayment is not made the difference between the minimum requirement and the actual repayment will be included in the taxpayers income for that year.

Homebuyers are precluded from deducting from income any RRSP contributions that are withdrawn to fund a homebuyers plan within 90 days of deposit.

Any funds withdrawn from an RRSP forego the tax-deferred income that those funds would earn, however, this disadvantage must be weighed against the benefit of homeownership and a tax-free capital gain that can accrue on an individual's principal residence. In fact, like many retirees who at some point downsize their principal residence, the individual may be better off buying the home as soon as possible. At retirement, downsizing the home generates tax-free capital, which can at that point be reinvested to produce additional income and may in fact produce a better situation than that of having pretax funds tied up within the RRSP.

6. **Lifelong Learning Plan. (LLP)**

Beginning in 1999 individuals will be able to withdraw up to $20,000 from their RRSPs on a tax-free basis to finance full-time educational retraining for themselves or for their spouses. These withdrawals can be structured with the maximum of $10,000 being withdrawn annually. Repayments must begin no later than 60 days after the 5th year following the first withdrawal and must be repaid in equal installments over a 10-year period.

7. **Tax efficiency.**

For many individuals and couples, RRSPs represent the majority of their investment assets. When these RRSPs are eventually matured all of the income that is produced, is fully taxable and this income is taxed at the individuals marginal tax rate. Where possible, investments such as interest-bearing deposits, CPB's, T-bills, and bonds are most advantageously held within the tax-sheltered structure of the RRSP. Investments for which preferential tax treatment exists, such as common stock (capital gains) and preferred shares (dividends), should be held, where possible, outside of the RRSP in order to reap the maximum benefits afforded to investors under the *Income Tax Act*, for these types of income.

An individual who holds cash in a self-directed RRSP and securities outside of the RRSP should consider the possibility of a swap of the assets. Although there may be income taxes triggered on this deemed disposition, this tactic allows the individual to continue to hold the securities and places cash in hand which can be used for other purposes, such as reducing debt on which interest is not deductible.

The value of the tax deferral gained by using an RRSP depends on an individual's age, time until withdrawal, and tax bracket. Generally speaking, it requires a long holding period for dividend or capital gain producing securities held within an RRSP to offset the higher income taxes that will be applicable when the income from the securities is finally withdrawn from the RRSP.

Labour Sponsored Venture Capital Corporations (LSVCC) provide venture capital for small to medium-sized Canadian businesses. LSVCCs are investment funds that are sponsored by labour organizations. To stimulate venture capital creation, the federal and provincial governments provide tax credits to investors in LSVCCs and in most provinces, these vehicles can be held within one's RRSP.

Individuals investing in LSVCCs receive a federal tax credit of 15% of the cost of the investment and the maximum federal tax credit is $750. Some provinces have matching credits that increase the total credits available to $1,500 for a $5,000 purchase of LSVCC shares.

If purchased through an RRSP, the tax benefits are significant. For example, a $5,000 contribution to an RRSP is deductible under the regular RRSP rules, and the individual also receives the LSVCC tax credits. Depending on the province, and assuming a marginal tax rate of 50%, an individual purchasing $5,000 of LSVCC shares in an RRSP saves about $4,000 in tax.

Additionally, recent amendments allow investors who own LSVCCs within their RRSPs the ability to increase the maximum amount of foreign content allowed within the RRSP. With this current change, for each $1 invested in an LSVCC, investors can hold an additional $3 of foreign content to an overall maximum of 40% of the RRSP's book value.

8. **Borrowing to contribute to an RRSP.**

As a rule, interest expense that is incurred on funds borrowed to purchase income-earning investments is deductible for income tax purposes. Revenue Canada requires a reasonable expectation of future income potential from the investment, which is greater than the interest expense claimed. Income for this purpose includes interest and dividends; it does not include capital gains.

Conversely, interest on funds that are borrowed to make an RRSP investment is not deductible for income tax purposes. Some individuals argue that it is preferable to borrow rather than to forego the current tax year's RRSP contribution. This is a form of forced savings. This strategy is most effective if the tax refund generated by the RRSP contribution is used to retire the loan as soon as possible. One of the major benefits that make RRSPs so attractive is the reinvestment of the tax savings. Taxpayers, who borrow therefore, are missing out on a major component of the total return and benefit from the RRSP vehicle. A powerful argument can be made that these individuals would be further ahead in the long run, to make monthly contributions to the RRSP rather than to make monthly payments on the loan. However, given the stock market returns which Canadians have enjoyed over the last decade, the legions of dedicated sales people who have espoused the use of debt, huge advertising campaign's every winter (RRSP season) by the financial institutions, and the availability of easy credit, this argument for the most part has been ignored or at best it has been relegated to the background.

Registered Retirement Savings Plan (RRSP) maturity options

The longer that an individual can delay taking income from the RRSP, the longer the time frame available for the funds to compound and to continue to grow. It may be prudent to derive income from non-registered investment funds before depleting registered sources in order to maximize the tax-deferred compounding.

Nevertheless, at some point and by the end of the year in which an individual turns age 69 at the latest, there is a requirement to mature the funds held within an RRSP. If the decision regarding the maturation of the RRSP is not taken by the annuitant at age 69, Revenue Canada will make the decision for them. Although age 69 is the deadline for the maturation of an RRSP, funds can be withdrawn from the plan anytime beforehand.

Eventually as funds are withdrawn from the RRSP, income taxes are payable.

There are three methods by which funds in an RRSP can be matured:

(1) Cash withdrawal,

(2) Annuities, or

(3) Registered Retirement Income Fund (RRIF).

(1) **Cash withdrawal.**

Cash withdrawal is the method that Revenue Canada deems to be the maturation option unless otherwise specified by the annuitant. Any amounts withdrawn in cash from an RRSP must be included in income in the year of withdrawal. All withdrawals from an RRSP are taxed as ordinary income even if the funds were accumulated as capital gains or from dividends. Partial withdrawals from an RRSP plan are permitted and these partial withdrawals do not deregister the entire plan.

Lump sum cash withdrawals from an RRSP are subject to withholding tax. Withdrawals of up to $5,000 are subject to withholding tax of 10% (25% in Quebec). Withdrawals of up to $15,000 are assessed withholding taxes of 20% (33% in Quebec), and withdrawals of more than $15,000 are subject to withholding tax of 30% (38% in Quebec). Withholding taxes are applied against the actual amount of income tax owed by the taxpayer, which will depend upon other sources of income for the tax year.

Although cash withdrawals from an RRSP are certainly an allowable option, this is the least attractive method of maturing an RRSP from a tax efficiency perspective.

(2) **Annuities.**

Funds held within an RRSP can be used to purchase an annuity. The amount of income paid from the annuity will depend upon the value of the funds to be invested, current market interest rates, the age of the annuitant, and type of annuity payout option which is purchased.

RRSP funds can be used to purchase life only annuities, joint survivor annuities, or a life annuity with a guarantee period (refund annuity). These are identical annuity options to those described previously under the maturation of registered pension plans.

Additionally, RRSP funds can be used to purchase a term certain annuity (TCA) which are also known as fixed term annuities. A TCA will provide an income stream up to the age of 90, or until the spouse is age 90.

Annuities offer the advantage of predictable and stable income that is guaranteed for the length of time that is specified in the particular annuity contract that is chosen. This advantage is particularly evident to individuals who purchased life annuities during the early 1980s when interest rates reached 18%, and who have watched interest rates subsequently plummet. Life annuities also offer the distinct advantage, of a lifetime of guaranteed income that can never be outlived.

Annuities have a number of drawbacks. Once the decision has been taken to annuitize the RRSP funds, the decision is irrevocable and the contract cannot be altered in any way. Subject to the guarantee's that are offered by CompCorp with respect to annuity income, the safety of the investment income depends upon a strong issuing company. Annuities are illiquid and, depending upon the option chosen, principal and earnings can be lost in the event of the pre-mature death of the annuitant.

(3) **Registered Retirement Income Fund (RRIF).**

Registered retirement income funds (RRIFs) are fundamentally the extension of an RRSP. A RRIF enables an individual to continue to control, and to continue compounding, on a tax-deferred basis, the investment of retirement assets after the age of 69. Funds are easily transferred from an RRSP to the RRIF, which continues to hold investments, or assets that are identical to those which are considered to be qualifying investments for RRSP purposes. Capital must be paid out of a RRIF at least annually, subject to Revenue Canada's rules that require a specified minimum income must be withdrawn each year.

The minimum amount, which must be withdrawn from a RRIF in any particular year, is that stipulated percentage that is based upon the annuitant's age; the minimum withdrawal increases over time. The age that is used to determine the minimum withdrawal can be either the age of the annuitant or it may be based upon the age of the annuitant's spouse. If the couple have other sources of retirement income, basing the minimum withdrawal on the age of the youngest spouse ensures that income taxes are minimized.

RRIFs offer the advantage of control and flexibility. A RRIF, like an RRSP, can be self-directed with all investment decisions and choices controlled by the annuitant. A RRIF does not stipulate the maximum withdrawal, therefore funds can be withdrawn at anytime and in any amount that the annuitant sees fit (subject to Revenue Canada's minimum withdrawal rules). Any withdrawals that exceed the specified minimum for any given age are subject to withholding tax at source.

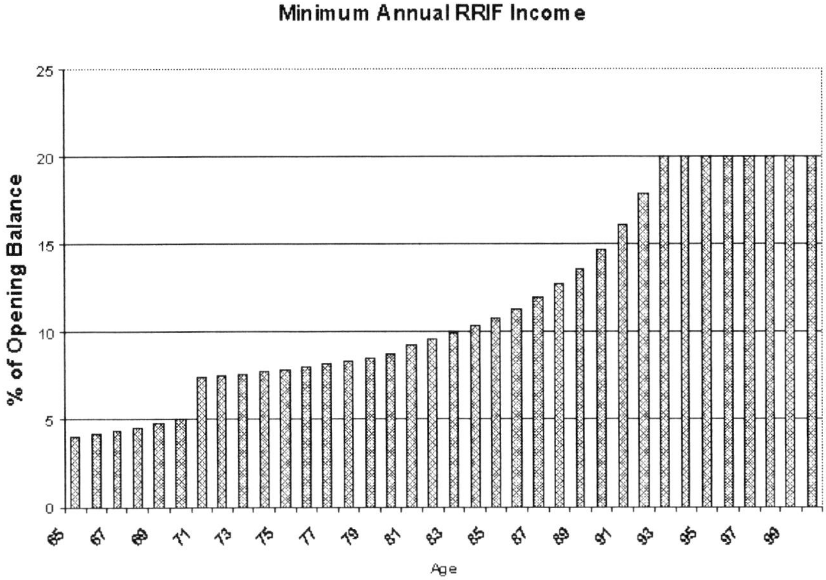

Retiring allowances

Retiring allowances are payments that are received by an employee in recognition of long service or alternatively these allowances are payments for loss of employment. Retiring allowances are normally fully taxable as ordinary income, however, the recipient may roll these monies, subject to certain restrictions, into an RRSP, in addition to the employee's annual deductible RRSP limit.

The maximum retiring allowance that can be rolled into an RRSP is $2,000 for each year, or part year, of employment prior to 1996 with the employer who is paying the retiring allowance. An additional $1,500 maybe rolled into an RRSP, for each year of employment before 1989 for which an employer's contributions to an RPP or DPSP had not yet vested in the employee. Starting in 1996, although the rollover's are still allowed, the limits will be restricted to years of employment before 1996. In order to avoid withholding taxes recipients of the retiring allowance should request that the employer directly transfer the funds to the RRSP.

Evaluating early retirement packages

Increases in global competitiveness and corporate cost reduction programs have made early retirement incentive packages commonplace in Canada in recent years. For some employees early retirement packages have been a boon that has allowed them to carry on a lifestyle similar to that which they enjoyed while working. For other employees early retirement can be a bane. Often the difference in the 2 situations can be directly attributable to a hasty acceptance or rejection of the proffered retirement package. Early retirement packages are usually complicated arrangements and typically, employees are given limited time in which to make a decision that will often impact the rest of their lives.

Considerations when evaluating a retirement package:

- What are the consequences if the package is not accepted?
- What type of pension plan does the employee belong to?
- What are the guarantees that are implicit in the pension plan?
- What are the actuarial assumptions upon which the pension benefits are based?
- How does the early retirement package compare with the benefits that the employee would have received at normal retirement age?
- Is the pension benefit indexed to inflation?
- Does the offer reduce penalties that are normally associated with the pension plan when the employee takes early retirement?
- Is there a retiring allowance available?
- How much of the retiring allowance can be rolled into an RRSP?
- Can the retiring allowance be structured in a manner such that income taxes are minimized?
- Are medical benefits included and for how long?
- Are any other benefits included in the package?
- What are the tax consequences of the early retirement package?
- Is the individual mentally prepared for the inevitable psychological impact of the transition from work life to retirement?
- Is the individual planning to return to the workforce by seeking other employment or starting a business?

Glossary

Actuary. A person who specializes in the mathematics of insurance and pension plans.

Actuarial valuation. An examination by an actuary to determine whether the assets and contributions to the pension plan will be sufficient to provide the promise pensions when due.

Annuitant. The one to whom an annuity or pension is payable.

Annuitize. To begin to receive a series of payments from capital that has accumulated in a pension plan or an annuity. The payments may be for a fixed or variable amount, and the time frame may be for a fixed period, or for variable periods such as a lifetime.

Annuity. A specific sum of money payable for a stated period. These contracts are usually sold by insurance companies, but may be available from other financial institutions. The income stream paid from an annuity usually begins at some time in the future. Either an annuity may be purchased with a single lump sum or the capital can be accumulated by paying a series of premiums.

Annuity certain or term certain annuity (TCA). An annuity payable at equal intervals during a stipulated period and not dependent upon a person's life span.

Commuted value. The single sum discounted at a given rate of interest that represents the present value of a stipulated number of instalments payable at fixed future dates. Often called the discounted value.

Cost of living adjustment (COLA). Any increase in annuity or pension benefits according to the rise in the consumer price index (CPI).

Deemed disposition. An income tax rule that requires that a disposition of property has taken place for the calculation of capital gains taxes, irrespective of an actual sale. For example, there is a deemed disposition upon death.

Disability pension. An annuity that is payable when an individual becomes disabled before normal retirement age.

Dividend Tax Credit (DTC). Revenue Canada's attempt to eliminate the double taxation of dividend income from taxable Canadian corporations. Dividends are grossed-up by 25% and a dividend tax credit of 13.33% is calculated on this grossed-up amount. The taxpayer claims this credit when determining federal and provincial taxes payable.

Early retirement age. The age established by the terms of a pension plan, which is earlier than normal retirement age, at which time an annuitant may receive benefits from the pension plan.

Forfeitures. Amounts contributed on behalf of terminated or non-vested pension plan participants. Such amounts are usually applied to reducing future employer contributions.

Funding. The process of setting aside money to pay retirement benefits.

Golden parachute. A substantial payment made to corporate executives when terminated.

Group RRSP. Type of retirement scheme similar to an RRSP in which contributions are deducted from one's payroll and are deposited directly into an RRSP account for the employee. These plans are administered by the employer and the employer may or may not contribute to the plan. Facilitates the employees ability to claim a reduction of withholding taxes at source.

Immediate vesting. A form of vesting under which rights to benefits are acquired immediately upon entry into the plan.

Integration with CPP. A registered pension plan usually provides a larger pension until the annuitant qualifies for the government benefits. At that time benefits from the registered pension plan are reduced by the amount of the government benefits. Integration therefore provides a level pension benefit throughout retirement.

Joint and last survivor annuity or Joint life annuity. An annuity contract on which an income is payable for the lifetimes of 2 named annuitant's.

Life annuity or single straight life annuity. An annuity on which the income is payable for the annuitant's life. No provision is made to return the unused portion of the premium.

Life expectancy. The length of time a person of a specified age is expected to live. Life expectancy is a statistical average based on mortality tables, which shows the rate of death at a given age.

Minimum funding. The minimum amount that must be contributed by an employer to a registered pension plan.

Normal retirement date. The earliest date at which an annuitant qualifies for a normal retirement pension.

Past service pension adjustment (PSPA). PSPA's can only occur under a defined benefit pension plan. When an employer upgrades or improves the defined benefit plan, the employer will often make additional contributions to an employee's plan in order to fund the improvements. The PSPA is the difference between the pension adjustment under the old plan and PA under the new plan.

Pension adjustment reversal (PAR). An adjustment that will restore the registered retirement savings plan (RRSP) contribution room to an individual who was previously an annuitant under a defined benefit pension plan and whose termination benefit is less than the participant's total pension adjustments (PAs) and past service pension adjustments (PSPAs).

Refund annuity. An annuity contract that provides for a lifetime of income to the annuitant. It also provides that a certain, minimum guaranteed amount will be paid to the annuitant or to the annuitant's beneficiary.

Retiring allowance. Amount paid by an employer at termination in recognition of long service.

Severance pay. A lump sum payable to an employee. Often paid in lieu of notice.

Vesting. Employee's right to receive a future pension vests when it is no longer contingent upon continued employment in the service of a specific employer.

Yearly maximum pensionable earnings (YMPE). Maximum amount of annual earnings, prior to reduction of the yearly basic earnings (YBE), upon which benefits from the Canada Pension Plan (CPP) are based.

Questions

1) When should one apply for OAS and CPP?

Individuals may apply for Canada Pension Plan and Old Age Security as early as one year in advance but one should apply at least six months before the commencement of the pension.

2) A homemaker has worked in the home during her/his working life. Will she/he receive OAS and CPP?

The Canada Pension Plan is a contributory, earnings based program and individuals will only receive CPP if they have contributed.

In order to receive OAS however, previous employment is not a requirement in determining eligibility, nor is it necessary to be retired. Age and residence in Canada are the relevant factors.

3) A self-employed person has limited income. Are they able to contribute additional amounts to the Canada Pension Plan so that they will be eligible for higher CPP payments upon retirement?

The CPP retirement pension is based on how much, and for how long, contributions have been made to the plan. It is also based upon the age at which one retires.

The Canada Pension Plan calculates the pension benefit by making adjustments before calculating the earnings which one contributed, over a career. Some lower earning periods may be eliminated, which serves to increase the amount of the pension benefit.

4) How much are the contributions into the Canada Pension Plan?

The amount paid is based on salary and CPP contribution limits. If self-employed, it is based on net business income after expenses. Contributions are not required on any other source of income, such as investment earnings.

5) A company does not have a registered pension plan. How can one ensure that they will have enough savings for retirement?

Under these circumstances, it is recommended that individual's plan ahead and forecast their retirement needs. Generally this can be accomplished by saving through RRSPs and investments held outside of RRSPs.

6) What is an individual pension plan (IPP)?

An individual pension plan is a defined benefit pension plan for one or more individuals. Typically, it is installed for the owner of a private company.

7) Who does the Guaranteed Income Supplement (GIS) benefit?

The GIS provides a benefit to low-income seniors based upon their income and marital status and is included with the monthly Old Age Pension payment.

Individuals are eligible to receive the Guaranteed Income Supplement if they are receiving an Old Age Security pension and:

- are single, separated, widowed or divorced and their previous years' income, is less than $11,736; or
- the individual and their spouse are both receiving the Old Age Security pension and have a combined yearly income, less than $15,312; or

- the spouse is not a pensioner and is not eligible for a Spouse's Allowance and the combined yearly income, is less than $28,416; or
- the spouse is 60 to 64 years of age and the combined yearly income, is less than $28,416. In this case, the spouse may also be eligible for a spouse's allowance.

8) How is the Guaranteed Income Supplement calculated?

One's income as well as marital status determines how much Guaranteed Income Supplement one is eligible to receive. If married or living in a common-law arrangement, the combined income of both spouses is used to calculate the benefit.

9) What is the Spouse's Allowance?

The Spouse's Allowance is based upon one's income. It is a monthly benefit paid to low income spouses in the 60 to 64 age brackets.

CHAPTER 5

Basic Economic Concepts

An understanding of the national and international economic environment is very important in preparing to make and implement financial decisions. The following basic economic concepts will help the investor to assess the economic environment before committing to a retirement or investment plan.

Gross domestic product and gross national product

Gross domestic product (GDP) is a measure of the goods and services produced by labor and property that is **located in Canada.** For the purposes of the GDP calculation, it does not matter whether Canadian residents own the resources; it matters only that the labor and other resources are **located in Canada.** GDP is the most common measure or international standard of national economic performance that is used by governments and economists worldwide.

Gross national product (GNP) is a measure of the goods and services that are produced by labor and property that is **supplied by Canadian residents.** It does not matter whether or not the laborers or the property is actually located in Canada, so long as the resources are **owned by Canadians.**

Since there is more foreign investment (particularly U.S.) in Canada than there is Canadian investment abroad, Canadian GDP is much larger than Canadian GNP. By way of contrast, for the U.S., GDP and GNP are nearly identical.

The economy's ability to produce is measured by its potential GDP. The growth in potential GDP is a function of:

- **The growth rate of the labor force.** The growth rate of the labor force is determined by demographics (birth rate, death rate, and immigration), and labor force participation rates (the percentage of the population that chooses to work).
- **The growth rate in the number of hours worked per worker.** The growth rate in the number of hours worked is determined by societal attitudes towards work and leisure.
- **The growth rate of productivity.** Productivity growth rate is a function of the technology used, innovation, social attitude, competition, resource utilization, and the skill of the labor force.

Supply and Demand

The demand for a product is defined as the quantity of the product which consumers are willing to purchase.

Factors that affect the demand relationship of a product include:

- **The price of the product.** Generally, the higher the product is priced, the lower the quantity demanded by consumers.
- **Consumer income.** The higher the consumer's income, the more goods the consumer will demand.
- **The price and availability of related goods.** If attractive substitute products are available at a lower price, less of a product will be in demand.
- **Consumer expectations.** If consumers expect product prices to rise, the more of the product they will demand now.
- **Advertising.** Effective advertising can promote and expand demand for the product of a company, or advertising can expand the marketplace for an entire industry.
- **Demographics.** As the population demographics change over the years so do consumer tastes and the products that they consume.

The demand curve for a product portrays the important relationship that exists between the quantity of a product that would be purchased and the prices that are charged for the product. Movement along the demand curve reflects a change in the quantity demanded. For example when prices decline, the quantity of the product demanded by consumers will increase. This is called the law of demand, and explains why demand curves normally slope downward and to the right. When the demand curve shifts, this is known as a change in demand. Change in demand is caused by some factor other than price.

The price elasticity of demand refers to the responsiveness of the quantity of goods that are demanded in relation to changes in the price of the product. Most products have elastic demand. Demand is said to be elastic when a given change in price produces a greater percent change in the quantity of the product that is demanded. The elasticity of demand is determined by the availability of substitute products and the percentage of the consumers total budget that is spent on the product. Necessities, in general, tend to be more inelastic than luxury goods. Gasoline represents a good example of a product with elastic demand. On the other hand, some products will be in demand no matter what the price; for example, insulin, which is used by diabetics. If the price of insulin were to double, in all probability the quantity of insulin demanded would remain constant. This situation is known as inelastic demand.

The supply of a product is defined as the quantity of the product which producers or manufacturers are willing to produce and sell.

A change in supply is different from the change in the quantity supplied. A **change in the quantity supplied** occurs when the price of the product itself changes, and this change is depicted as a movement along the existing supply curve. A **change in supply** occurs because of factors other than price. A change in supply is reflected by a movement or shift, of the entire supply curve, up or down.

The factors that affect supply changes, and which can shift the supply curve include:

- A change in the price of the inputs of production such as raw materials, labor, or capital.
- Changes in production technology such as the use of additional or more efficient machinery or production methods.
- Changes in fiscal or monetary policy such as the imposition of taxes or other incentives or disincentives introduced by governments.
- Natural disasters such as fires, floods, ice storms, or tornadoes which reduce the availability of goods on hand and may interrupt production schedules.

Profit is the major determinant of a supply curve. Therefore, an important factor that affects the supply curve is production cost. The law of supply says that, in the short run, producers will manufacture more of the product at higher prices. Supply curves normally slope upward and to the right. This relationship exists because companies will only produce more of a given product if the price at which they can sell the product covers the cost of production and yields a profit.

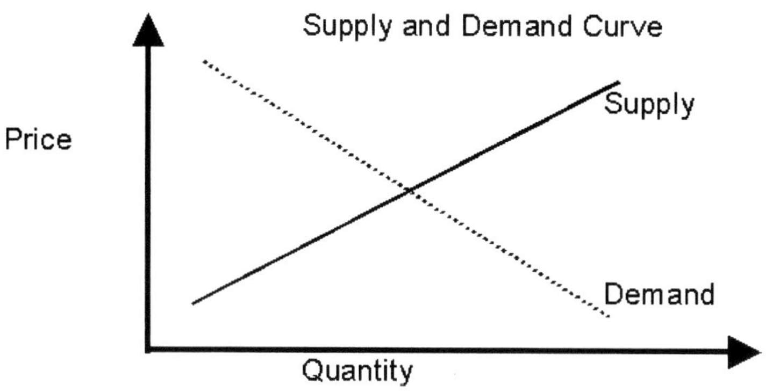

Interest rates and yield curves

Arguably, interest rates are the singular most important factor, which affect securities markets and investments. Interest rates can be thought of as the cost or price of money and therefore, interest rates have a powerful effect on the Canadian economy as follows:

- **The cost of capital**, which impacts on business investments and capital spending. A decrease in interest rates will often encourage business to expand by increasing production capability and modernizing manufacturing facilities with funds borrowed at a low interest cost.

- **Current consumer consumption.** Low and falling interest rates encourage consumers to spend and many borrow therefore increasing their current consumption of goods and services, particularly relatively expensive goods such as automobiles and appliances.

- **Savings rates of individuals.** Rising interest rates encourage consumers to save rather than to consume.

- **The discretionary spending habits of consumers.** Rising interest rates increase the cost of borrowing thereby increasing debt servicing costs. Rising debt service cost means that there is less discretionary income to be used for current consumption.

The level of interest rates in a closed economy that does not engage in trade with foreigners, is determined primarily by the supply and demand for credit (loanable funds). The supply of loanable funds is determined by savers who invest their money, which is then, in turn, loaned to consumers. The willingness to save is based upon the individual's willingness to trade current consumption for future consumption. The price demanded for this tradeoff is the interest rate.

The demand for loanable funds is a function of the desire for current consumption, and the lower the cost or interest rate, the greater the demand for loanable funds.

Creditors will consider a debtor's credit risk in establishing the interest rate to be charged. Specifically, the higher the risk of default the higher the interest rate charged. Additionally, if a creditor believes that inflation will rise over the term of the loan, the nominal interest rate charged for the loan will be increased so that the debt will be repaid in real dollars.

In a free market open economy which engages in international trading, the level of interest rates, in addition to the domestic supply and demand factors just discussed, is also impacted by:

- **Central bank operations.** Central banks can influence short-term interest rates through money-market operations.
- **The foreign exchange rate.** If interest rates are higher in the U.S. than in Canada, investment funds will flow to the U.S. (money goes where money grows) which may force the Bank of Canada to protect the Canadian dollar by raising short-term interest rates.
- **Central bank credibility.** If central bank policy is to keep inflation low and under control, interest rates can remain low.

The yield curve is a graphic representation of the relationship that exists between short and long-term interest rates at different points in time over the business cycle. Changes in the level of interest rates can dramatically affect both the price and the demand for debt securities. The bellwether or benchmark that is used to establish the level of interest rates in the Canadian economy is the federal government's treasury bills (T-bills) and bond issues. Under everyday and commonplace conditions, usually long-term interest rates are higher than short-term interest rates. When interest rates are plotted on a graph against the term to maturity, the resulting depiction of the term structure for interest rates is known as a normal yield curve. When short-term rates are higher than long-term rates, the yield curve is said to be inverted. The yield curve will often be inverted at the peak of an economic cycle because the Bank of Canada will attempt to slowdown the pace of economic activity by manipulating short-term interest rates upwards, through its intervention in the money-market and other open market operations.

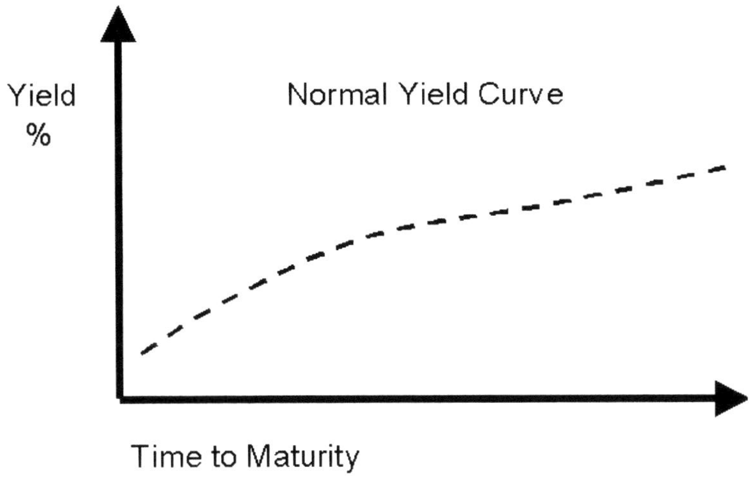

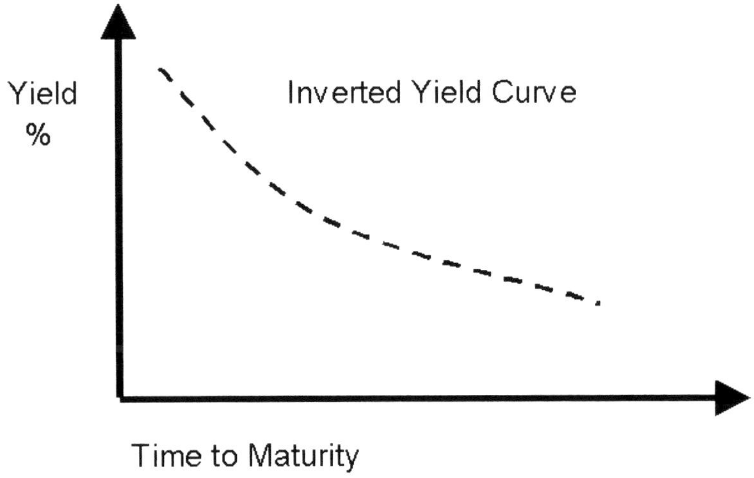

The term structure of interest rates is described by different theories, which attempt to elucidate the shape of the yield curve.

- **Segmented market theory.** This theory states that different participants in the bond market tend to concentrate their activities into the particular maturity segments, which most closely match their needs. Although this theory can explain any shape of yield curve, it is based on the unrealistic assumption that the market participants will *never move out* of their preferred segment no matter what the interest rate.

- **Preferred habitat theory.** This theory states that investors and borrowers prefer to invest in certain maturity segments along the yield curve. The theory states that investors will shift out of their preferred maturity segment (habitat) if they are rewarded for the risk of doing so, by higher interest rates.

- **Pure expectations theory.** This theory states that the yield curve adjusts to the participants expectations regarding what the market believes that interest rates will be in the future. If the market expects interest rates to rise, the yield curve should be positively sloped and if the market expects that interest rates will fall, the yield curve will be inverted.
- **Liquidity theory.** The liquidity theory is based upon an investors aversion to risk. This theory states that short-term rates should be lower than long-term rates because the long-term bond rates must include a premium for their lack of liquidity. The liquidity theory claims that the yield curve should therefore, always be positively sloped.
- **Biased expectation theory.** This theory combines both the pure expectations and liquidity theories. This theory can explain any shape of yield curve and because of the liquidity preference there is a natural bias towards a positive slope.

Inflation

The Bank of Canada defines inflation as the persistent rise in the cost of living over time.

The most common measure of inflation is the consumer price index (CPI). The CPI measures the cost each month to buy a basket of consumer goods. This basket of goods supposedly represents the same goods that typically would be purchased by an average family. The calculation of the CPI assumes that the same type and quantity of goods are purchased each month or each year, and the price of this basket of goods is compared and measured relative to a predefined base period. Another important indicator of inflation, are the settlements of collective agreements for unionized employees wage demands.

The economic consequences of inflation include:

- The erosion of the standard of living of those collecting and living on fixed incomes.
- Debtors benefit since loans are repaid with cheaper future dollars.
- Higher interest rates, which often translate into recessions.

- A transfer of wealth from the public to the government, if the government is a major debtor, and if the tax system is progressive and it is not indexed to inflation.

Unemployment

One on the goals of economic policy is to produce and maintain full employment. Full employment does not mean zero unemployment. There will always be a certain number of unemployed persons in the Canadian economy for various reasons.

- **Frictional unemployment** refers to individuals who are unemployed because they are voluntarily between jobs. Certain demographic sectors of the labor market change jobs more often than others. Young people for example, tend to have higher unemployment rates as they search for "better jobs".
- **Structural unemployment** refers to the individuals who are displaced because their skills are no longer in demand due to advances in technology or to societal changes. The advent of the automobile, for example, which created jobs for mechanics, displaced and eventually eliminated jobs for horse carriage makers.
- **Cyclical unemployment** refers to the normal waxing and waning in the unemployment rate that occurs due to the normal fluctuations during a business cycle.

The business cycle

An understanding of the business cycle helps an investor to focus on the "big picture", and is essential in order to set both short and long-term investment strategies and policies.

Business activity can be classified as having seasonal variations, cyclical fluctuations, and long-term secular trends. In addition, the economy and business activity can be affected by random and unexpected occurrences such as a war or "Asian flu". Over the long run, the Canadian economy has continued to expand and grow. However, this long-term growth has been volatile at times and the economy has experienced periodic fluctuations, which are known as the business cycle. There are no firm rules for identifying recessions; however, Statistics Canada defines a recession as 2 consecutive quarters of declining GDP growth. Although each business cycle is itself unique, most business cycles follow a more or less predictable pattern.

Although no business cycle will exactly match the previous cycle, some similarities and general conclusions can be drawn with respect to business and economic cycles and investment strategies in general. These strategies and phases can be tracked by watching certain economic indicators.

- **Leading** economic indicators tend to anticipate the health of the general economy and include: building permits issued, housing starts, manufacturer's new orders for durable goods, stock prices, average number of hours worked per week, and commodity prices.
- **Coincident** economic indicators change at approximately the same time and in the same direction as the overall economy. Examples of coincident economic indicators include: GDP, industrial production, personal income, and retail sales.
- **Lagging** indicators tend to change after the economy has turned and include: the unemployment rate, labor costs, inventory levels, and the rate of inflation.

The business cycle consists of four segments, which can be identified by the following signs or signals:

1) Recovery and expansion.

Inflation is stable, or rising only slightly. Typically, these stages last longer than the contraction phase.

Businesses are investing in new capacity to meet increased consumer demand. Corporate profits are rising because profit margins are increasing. Business is confident about the future and is planning production increases. New business start-ups outnumber bankruptcies. Inventories are under control. Retail sales are healthy.

Unemployment is steady or falling. Job creation is strong. Personal incomes are rising. Consumer confidence is high. Demand for credit is high. Consumer spending and housing construction fuels increasing economic activity.

Confidence is high and expectations become excessively optimistic. Investors are told that this time the world is different and that the trees will in fact "grow to the sky".

Typically, in the late stages of the expansion phase the central bank will start to tighten credit in an attempt to cool the economy off by raising short-term interest rates.

Stock and bond markets are booming.

Investment strategy at this point in the business cycle is to stop buying common stocks because the expansion, at some point, must end.

2) Peak.

Optimism and overconfidence override prudence and caution. Stock market and other economic indices are higher than the long-term trends.

Inflation is rising quickly caused by wage increases, labor shortages and product shortages. The pace of economic activity is high and efficiency starts to wane.

Business revenues are down, profits are falling. Production costs are rising faster than prices, which causes profit margins to shrink. Business is no longer making large capital investment. Business output typically exceeds sales. Inventories start to build up due to falling sales. Accounts receivable start to rise, which causes a shortage of working capital and this forces businesses to seek bank financing. Business confidence erodes.

Consumer confidence declines, housing sales fall, and big-ticket consumer spending drops as consumers worry about the future.

Central banks intervene to control inflation, by raising short-term interest rates, often causing inverted yield curves at this point in the cycle. Monetary policy bias is towards tightening credit, aimed at causing the economy to slow.

Rising interest rates cause bond prices to fall. Stock prices have weakened and stock market activity drops off. New stock and bond issues are poorly accepted by investors and become rare.

The investment strategy at this point in the cycle is to sell stocks of companies in cyclical industries, stocks with high P/E ratios, and low yielding stocks. Profits earned in the rising stock market should be invested in short term paper such as T-bills or money-market funds, which benefit from rising interest rates.

3) Recession or contraction.

When a recession is apparent, economically, the outlook is gloomy. This phase is shorter in duration than the expansion phase normally is.

Corporate profits are falling. Business failures increase. Industrial production falls. Business confidence deteriorates.

Unemployment rises. Consumer confidence falls. Consumers stop spending and become more cautious. New home construction falls. Personal bankruptcies rise. The nightly News and newspapers are pessimistic about the future.

Stock market activities weaken and decline.

The central bank is using lower interest rates and is encouraging credit granting in order to attempt to stimulate economic activity.

The investment strategy at this point in the cycle is to sell short-term bonds and to buy mid and long-term bonds which will benefit from falling interest rates.

4) Trough.

The end of the recession is apparent and gradually conditions that are more favorable start to surface. Stock and bond indices are below the long-term trends. The rate of the deterioration of the economy starts to slow. The leading economic indicators are improving and signs of stability start to return.

Production output is low. Business sales are depressed. Business outlook is pessimistic. There is minimal new capital investment. Inventories have declined.

Unemployment is high. Personal income is down which causes reduced consumption. Consumer confidence is low. Doom and gloom are rampant. "The sky is falling".

However, the inflation rate is falling along with interest rates. Labor is plentiful. Pent-up demand starts to build in the economy. Typically, raw material prices have fallen. Slowly, business and consumer confidence starts to rise.

At this point in the cycle, the central bank is attempting to stimulate economic growth by easing credit. Short-term interest rates are reduced in an attempt to restart the economy.

The investment strategy at this point in the cycle is to sell long-term bonds. Profits from long-term bonds should be repositioned by purchasing common stocks of cyclical industries that have fallen out of favor.

The Phases of the Business Cycle

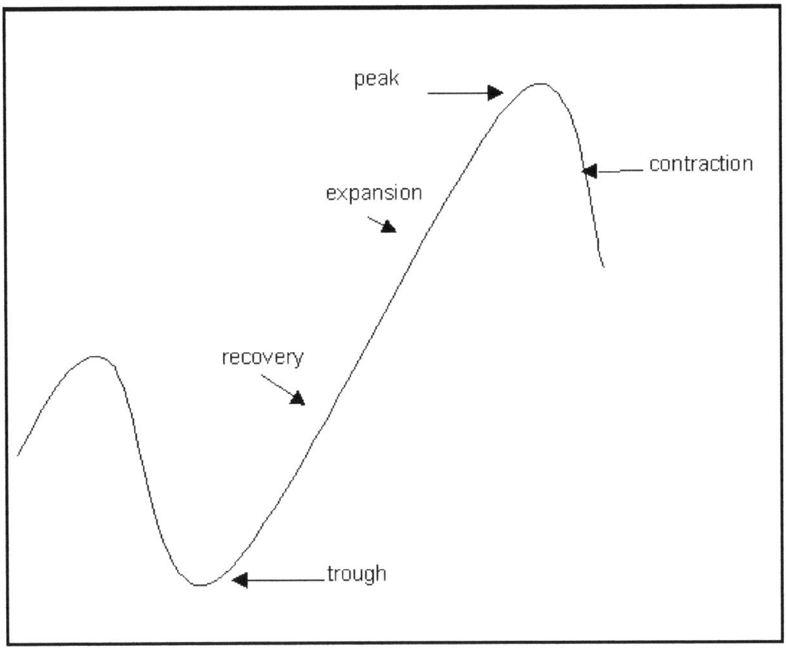

The Bank of Canada

The Bank of Canada (the Bank) is Canada's central bank. It is known as the banker's bank since the Bank of Canada does not receive retail deposits from consumers, but does hold the deposits of financial institutions and governments. The Bank of Canada was created by an act of Parliament in 1934 and commenced operations in 1935. Since 1938, the Minister of Finance has held all of the share capital of the Bank of Canada.

According to the *Bank of Canada Act*, the Bank has four primary functions:

- **Monetary policy** — Monetary policy is concerned with the Canadian standard of living. The Bank's mandate is to keep the economy on a slow, stable, steady expansion and to promote full employment. The bank implements monetary policy using interest rates, the exchange rate of the Canadian dollar, and the rate of growth of the money supply.
- **Currency in circulation** — The Bank of Canada is responsible for the currency notes and coins that are circulating in the Canadian

economy. The Bank deals with crimes of counterfeiting because part of its job is to maintain the integrity of our currency.

- **Central banking services** — The Bank of Canada is the banker for the federal government and for other financial institutions. The Bank operates in the Canadian money markets every day, and controls the payment clearing system. Monetary policy is implemented through these open market operations.
- **Debt management** — The Bank of Canada acts as the government's fiscal agent. As their fiscal agent, they are the advisors to the federal government on debt matters, foreign exchange and monetary policy.

The most visible and important of the Bank of Canada's functions is that of implementing monetary policy. The Bank's principal task when implementing monetary policy is to determine the optimum rate of growth of the money supply. This task is complicated and the Bank must distinguish between monetary needs which arise from seasonal trends in the economy, changes in the business cycle, and needs which arise due to unexpected, and usually externally induced shocks to the Canadian economy such as "the Asian flu". The Bank of Canada has a variety of means at its disposal with which to implement monetary policy.

These methods include:

- Changes to the Bank of Canada rate.
- Open market operations in the Canadian money market.
- Transfer of Government of Canada deposits through the drawdown and redeposit mechanism.
- Short-term advances (loans) to financial institutions and money-market dealers, which are often called overnight money.
- Varying the chartered bank's required reserve ratios, which affect the ease with which credit is made available.
- Moral suasion which is an informal request to the financial institutions to either ease or tighten credit, and is also known as "jaw-boning".

The best known of the Bank's monetary policy tools is the setting of the Bank of Canada Rate. The Bank of Canada Rate or Bank rate is the short-term lending rate charged by the Bank of Canada for advances made to financial institutions. The Bank rate is conveyed by the Bank's participation in the money markets. The money market is where short-term borrowers and lenders come together. Some examples of investments traded in the money market are Treasury Bills (T-bills), commercial paper and bankers acceptances.

Foreign exchange rates.

Global economic conditions affect Canadian companies selling products into foreign markets, as witnessed by the "Asian flu" and its damage to the BC economy in the late 1990s. Additionally, the globalization of business may introduce new competitors and trading partners.

The Canadian economy is unquestionably highly dependent upon foreign trade. This dependence on trading means that the value of the Canadian dollar is vitally important to the livelihood and living standards of millions of Canadians. The foreign exchange marketplace is global in scope and foreign exchange rates are based on the supply and demand for a particular currency. In the international foreign exchange markets, currencies are traded around the clock and the accepted convention is that all foreign exchange rates are established or measured relative to the U.S. dollar, which is considered to be the international standard.

In the international arena, a country may employ either a fixed or a floating exchange rate system. Under a fixed exchange rate system the currency is pegged against other currencies, usually by imposing currency controls which preclude the citizens from holding foreign currencies; or the central bank will take measures to ensure that the currency stays within a fixed range by purchasing or selling currency in the foreign exchange market. Currently, an example of the fixed exchange rate system is the Hong Kong dollar.

A floating exchange rate means that the central bank will only intervene in the foreign exchange marketplace when it considers the movement of the currency to be excessive. Central banks can either buy or sell in the foreign exchange market, or they can manipulate short-term interest rates. The Canadian dollar has been freely floating since the 1950s. When the Canadian dollar is under downward pressure, the Bank of Canada will intervene in the foreign exchange market by purchasing Canadian dollars in an attempt to increase the demand for the Canadian dollar and thereby attempting to support the value and strengthening of the dollar.

When the Canadian dollar is weak relative to the U.S. dollar, products produced in Canada are relatively inexpensive to an American consumer. In other words, a weak Canadian dollar benefits Canadian exporters. At the same time, a weak Canadian dollar means that products produced in the

U.S. are expensive when purchased by Canadians, which translates to mean that a weak Canadian dollar puts Canadian importers at a comparative disadvantage relative to their U.S. counterparts.

It is virtually impossible in Canada to read a business newspaper or listen to a newscast when there is not some mention that is made to the external value of the Canadian dollar.

Factors influencing the foreign exchange rate.

- **Monetary policy.** An easy monetary policy increases the money supply and tends to lower the currency's exchange rate. A tight monetary policy reduces the money supply and increases the exchange rate. It is the relative monetary policies between 2 countries that determines the relationship between the 2 currencies; therefore, from a foreign exchange perspective Canadian monetary policy can not be viewed in isolation.
- **Relative product prices.** If Canadian goods are relatively cheap, they will be in high demand. Purchasing power parity states that currency exchange rates adjust to the relative price levels or the expected inflation rates between 2 countries. Everything else being equal, the country with the lowest inflation rate, will have the strongest currency.
- **Relative income levels.** The higher the income levels are within a country, the more its people will tend to consume and the more they will desire imported goods. Therefore, the country with the highest real growth rates will tend to have the weakest currency because its people will spend a higher percentage of their disposable incomes to pay for imported goods.
- **Taste and quality considerations.** A country whose goods are considered to be of high quality, or whose goods are highly desirable, will tend to have the stronger currency.
- **Interest rate differentials.** The country with the highest real interest rate will attract foreign investment and therefore strengthen the currency.
- **Relative profit.** A country that offers high rates of return on equity investment, assuming equal risk, will attract foreign capital and thereby strengthen the currency.
- **Relative political risk.** A country that is viewed as a political safe haven tends to attract foreign capital, which serves to strengthen the currency.

- **Currency speculation.** Foreign currency speculators can cause changes in the supply and demand of a currency. These changes in supply and demand will translate into either a strengthening or a weakening of the currency.

When examined in isolation the effect of each of the above factors on the exchange rate seems obvious and straightforward. However, in the real world, these factors when considered together often obscure the resulting impact upon a currency.

Financial institutions

The world of investment has emerged as an important cornerstone in planning and organizing one's financial resources. Regulations and securities law are available in Canada to protect investors and to provide them with a level of confidence in their dealings with the domestic markets. A number of federal and provincial laws regulate the activities and actions of participants in the securities markets.

The Office of the Superintendent of Financial Institutions (OSFI) was established by legislation that merged the Department of Insurance and the Office of the Inspector General of Banks. This legislation established a single agency responsible for the regulation and supervision of Federally Regulated Financial Institutions (FRFIs). OSFI is also responsible for monitoring federally regulated pension plans. Other financial institutions and pension plans are provincially incorporated and are therefore not regulated by OSFI.

FRFIs include all banks, all federally incorporated or registered insurance, trust and loan companies, cooperative credit associations, and fraternal benefit societies. Although legislation, regulation, guidelines and policy statements affect how FRFIs conduct their business, day-to-day operations are not subject to government oversight. FRFI legislation and regulations are available at the Department of Justice's WebSite.

OSFI does not regulate the Canadian securities industry.

In Canada, the regulation of the securities business is a provincial responsibility.

Regulation of the primary and secondary securities markets has important consequences for investors.

The primary market is the market for new issues of securities, typically involving underwriters and corporate issuers.

The secondary market is the market where previously issued securities are traded, including both the organized exchanges and the over-the-counter (OTC) network. The OTC market is a computer and telephone network of securities dealers for the trading of securities not listed on other exchanges. Without the existence of an extensive investment dealer community and efficient and orderly security markets, the costs and risks involved in the issuing of securities would rise.

Glossary

Aggregate demand curve. Downward sloping curve, which indicates an inverse relationship between price and the total quantity of goods, or services, which will be purchased.

Aggregate supply curve. Upward sloping curve, which indicates a direct relationship between price and the total quantity of goods, or services, which will be produced.

Automatic stabilizers. Economic policies that automatically operate with the intent to promote stability in the economy without further changes in fiscal policy.

Average tax rate. Total direct income taxes divided by taxable income.

Balanced budget. The situation in which total government revenue exactly equals total government expenditure.

Balance of payments. A national account, which reflects the total of all payments, owed to foreigners and all of the payments that are received from foreigners.

Balance of trade. A national account, which is calculated as total merchandise exported minus total merchandise imported.

Bond. A bond is a marketable debt security that requires an issuer to pay a holder the par value, at a specified maturity date, and to make agreed upon, scheduled interest payments.

Budget deficit. Total government expenditures exceed total government revenue.

Business cycle. Regularly recurring stages in the fluctuations of the economy.

Business cycle indicators include leading, lagging and coincident. A leading indicator anticipates economic changes and moves before the economy changes. A lagging indicator follows the economy. A coincident indicator changes at the same time and directly with the economy.

Capital account. A national account, which records transactions with foreigners that, involves the ownership of financial assets.

Central bank. The generic name for the body established to regulate the national currency and monetary policy. In Canada, it is the Bank of Canada. In the United States, it is called the Federal Reserve Board.

Classical economists. Traditional school of macroeconomic belief which subscribes to the theory that market prices and wages would fall during recessions, and this alone would bring the economy back to full employment. Adam Smith was the first classical economist.

Closed economy. Economy which neither imports nor exports goods or services.

Competitive tender. A method used by the Bank of Canada to distribute new bond issues. In the tender process, the Bank of Canada requests bids from primary distributors and they award the securities for distribution to the highest bidder.

Consumer Price Index (CPI). An inflation indicator which measures changes in the cost of living by measuring the changes in price of a fixed basket or sample of goods.

Countercyclical policy. An economic policy that attempts to direct the economy in the opposite direction from the forces of the business cycle. For example, the stimulation of demand during the contraction phase of the business cycle.

Crowding out effect. Higher interest rates caused by federal government budget deficits that reduce or crowd out private spending.

Current account. A national account which records the cumulative total of goods and services, income from investments, and foreign aid exchanged.

Cyclical company. A firm whose earnings rise and fall with the economy, e.g., a mining company

Defensive stock. A stock whose return investors do not expect to decline as much as the overall market during a downturn or bear market. The stock of a company with a record of high-quality earnings and continuous dividend payments, which has shown relative stability in poor economic conditions, e.g. a utility company.

Deflation. Describes a decline of price levels in the economy.

Depression. An extended and extremely severe recession.

Disposable income. An individual's income after income taxes, which can be either consumed or saved.

Drawdown and Redeposit. A cash management tool used to implement monetary policy by the Bank of Canada. Through the management of liquid cash deposits in the banking system, drawdowns and redeposits are used to influence short-term interest rates.

Earnings multiplier or P/E ratio. Commonly used method of stock valuation that measures the relationship between a company's stock price and its earnings.

Economic policy. Programs intended to alleviate or avert a problem.

Equilibrium. A state that exists when opposing forces balance each other.

Excess reserves. When a financial institution holds more reserves than are legally required.

Exchange rate The price to exchange a local currency unit into a foreign currency.

Expansionary fiscal policy. An expansion of a budget deficit caused by increased government spending, a tax cut, or some combination of both.

External debt. Total national debt that is owed to foreigners.

Fiat money or legal tender. Paper currency or anything else, which is money because it has been decreed to be by the government.

Fiscal policy. Government tax and spend policies intended to influence the macroeconomy.

Fractional reserve banking. The banking system under which banks hold reserves which are less than 100% of the liabilities.

Free trade. Describes the condition under which firms of different nations trade without restrictions imposed by governments.

Fungible. Items that are easily exchanged for one another.

Gross domestic product (GDP). Total market value of all final goods and services produced in Canada during a fiscal year.

Gross national product (GNP). Total market value of all final goods services produced by Canadian residents.

Import quota. Government imposed barrier that restricts the quantity of a foreign good that may be imported.

Infrastructure. The legal, monetary, educational, transportation and communications systems that are necessary for the efficient operation of a modern open economy and which are usually provided by government.

Keynesian economics. Macroeconomic viewpoint introduced by Maynard Keynes, which concludes that fiscal and monetary policy should be used to promote full employment.

Law of comparative advantage. Asserts that specialization in the production of a good results in lower costs and therefore in the ability to benefit by exchanging those goods for other desired goods.

Law of demand. Economic principle which states that an inverse relationship exists between the price of the good and the quantity of the good that buyers are willing to purchase.

Law of supply. Economic principle describing the direct relationship between the price of a good, and the quantity that a supplier will offer for sale.

Macroeconomics. Economic principles that focus on the impacts to society in a large aggregate market such as the national economy as a whole.

Marginal propensity to consume (MPC). Change in current consumption divided by change in disposable income.

Marginal tax rate (MTR). Additional tax liability divided by additional income. For example, if $100 of additional income increases an individual's income taxes by $45, the marginal tax rate is 45%.

Means tested income transfers. Government transfers that are limited to individuals with income below a certain minimum stipulated level.

Microeconomics. Economic principles that focus on the societal impacts of the affairs of individual units such as a household or a business firm.

Monetarists. Descriptive term for economists who believe that the money supply is the most important factor affecting the economy.

Monetary policy. Macroeconomic goals that are achieved by the deliberate and planned manipulation of the money supply and credit offerings.

Money markets. are used for trading short-term debt instruments and operate through dealers around the world. New York is the leading money-market centre, followed by Tokyo and London. Dealers in the money markets are in constant communication with each other and with other participants such as major borrowers and institutional investors in order to take advantage of arbitrage opportunities. These practices improve market efficiency and transparency, which translates into more consistent global pricing.

Money supply. The amount of money in circulation as defined by the central bank.

Monopoly. Descriptive term for the market characterized by a single seller of a product for which there are no substitutes.

National debt. A running total of all previous federal budget deficits. The national debt represents the total sum of the accumulated indebtedness of the federal government.

Net exports. Exports minus imports.

New classical economists. Modern school of economic thought holding the belief that there are strong forces pushing a market economy toward full employment equilibrium. These economists believe that macroeconomic policy is an ineffective tool with which to reduce economic fluctuations.

Noncompetitive tender. Distribution method for Government of Canada bonds which is used by the Bank of Canada. The Bank of Canada allows primary distributors to request additional bonds at the tender price.

Oligopoly. Descriptive term for the market arrangement in which only a small number of producers exist in an industry.

Open economy. Economy that imports and exports goods and services.

Open market operations. One of the methods by which a central bank can influence interest rates. For example, the Bank of Canada can influence short-term interest rates by trading with the other parties in the money market.

Opportunity cost. The amount or cost of the best alternative that must be sacrificed in order to make another choice.

Personal consumption. Household spending on goods and services.

Personal income. Total of all income received by individuals before income taxes. Personal income must be used for consumption, saving, or the payment of taxes.

Planned economy. The economic system in which government determines the allocation of resources.

Price/earning (P/E ratio) or earnings multiplier. A valuation measure. The number by which earnings per share is multiplied to estimate a stock's value. Calculated as the common stock's current market price divided by its expected per share earnings.

Productivity. A measure of the average output produced per worker. Productivity is usually reported as hourly output per worker.

Protective tariff. A duty or tax on imports designed to protect domestic manufacturers from foreign competition.

Purchasing power parity. The theory that the exchange rate between 2 currencies is a function of the differences in inflation between 2 nations.

Pure competition. Descriptive term for a marketplace which consists of a large number of small firms in an industry.

Rationing. The allotment of a resource to its users who would like to have more of it. Price typically performs this allocation for consumer goods and services.

Real values. The resulting values that have been correctly adjusted for the effects of inflation.

Recession. A descriptive term for a downturn in economic activity which is usually accompanied by a rising unemployment rate. Typically, defined as 2 successive quarters of declining GDP.

Recognition lag. The time that elapses between when a policy change is needed in order to stabilize the economy, and the time when the need is recognized by the policymakers.

Reserves. The amount of cash that a chartered bank maintains in its vault plus amounts on deposit at the Bank of Canada.

Reverse special purchase and resale agreement or reverse SPRA. If the bank wants to raise overnight interest rates, it employs a mechanism known as a Reverse SPRA or Reverse. A reverse SPRA is the mirror image of the special. In a reverse, the Bank of Canada sells T-bills to the money-market dealers, and promises to buy them back the next day at some specified rate. A reverse effectively drains reserves from the system, which tightens credit and raises interest rates.

Secular trend. The long-term trend of expansion or contraction in the macroeconomy.

Special drawing rights (SDR). Established by the international monetary fund. SDR's are accounting entries that can be used by a country to make international account payments.

Special purchase and resale agreements (SPRA) or Special. Monetary policy tool of the Bank of Canada which is used to lower short-term interest rates (usually overnight), by adding reserves. It involves 2 simultaneous transactions. One transaction is the purchase of securities usually T-bills from a money-market dealer. The second transaction is an agreement by the dealer to repurchase the securities from the Bank of Canada the next day, at interest rates specified by the Bank of Canada.

Supply shock. Unexpected event that temporarily increases or decreases supply.

Supply side economics. School of macroeconomic thought who hold the belief that supply is greatly affected by changes in costs, particularly the marginal tax rate.

Tariff. A tax or duty imposed on imports.

Term structure of interest rates. The relationship between the term to maturity and yield to maturity for a sample of comparable bonds at a given time. Popularly known as the yield curve.

Transfer payment or subsidy. Federal government funds paid to individuals and provinces for which nothing is supplied in return by the recipient.

Treasury Bills or (T-bills). Short-term obligations issued in large denominations. They are negotiable, bearer instruments issued by the Government of Canada or by a Canadian province. T-bills do not pay interest. Alternatively, they are sold at a discount and mature at par. Treasury bills issued by the federal government are considered the highest quality. They are usually issued for terms of 91, 182, and 364 days.

Utility. The satisfaction or gain which is expected to result from a choice or from a course of action.

Velocity of money. GDP divided by money supply. Represents the number of times a dollar is used to purchase finished goods or services in a year. The turnover rate of a dollar.

World trade organization (WTO). The entity which is responsible for monitoring and enforcing international trade agreements and the reduction of trade barriers among the member countries. Before 1994, the organization was known as the General Agreement on Tariffs and Trade (GATT).

Yield curve. A graphic presentation of various bond yields. The graph displays the term structure of interest rates by plotting the yields of all bonds of the same quality, with maturities ranging from the shortest to the longest available. The resulting curve shows if short-term interest rates are higher or lower than long-term interest rates. If short-term interest rates are lower, there is a positive or normal yield curve. If short-term rates are higher, a negative or inverted yield curve results. If there is little difference between short and long-term rates, there is a flat yield curve.

Yield spread. The difference in yield between various issues of securities. In comparing bonds, the yield spread usually refers to issues of different credit quality since issues of the same maturity and quality would normally have the same yields. The yield spread is a function of supply and demand, credit rating, and interest rates.

Questions

1) What is meant by the terms monetary and fiscal policy?

Monetary policy is the Canadian government's formal effort to manage money in the economy. The objectives of monetary policy are to realize specific economic goals such as economic growth, full employment, price stability, and protection of the value of the Canadian dollar. Monetary policy is carried out by the Bank of Canada. Fiscal policy is politician made discretionary policies, which involve the manipulation of government finances by the raising or lowering of taxes or government spending in order to promote economic stability and growth. Fiscal policy is carried out through politicians in the house of Parliament.

2) What are automatic stabilizers?

Automatic stabilizers are an economic mechanism, implemented by fiscal policy, which act to stabilize personal incomes as the economy fluctuates. In other words, automatic stabilizers act to cushion the economy. Examples of automatic stabilizers in Canada are Employment Insurance (EI), the progressive nature of the income tax system, and welfare.

3) What is money?

Money can be anything, so long as it serves three basic functions:

- Money acts as a medium of exchange with which to buy goods and services (money is fungible).
- Money acts as a store of value and can be used as a means of holding wealth.
- Money acts as a standard of value and the dollar is a convenient way of measuring value.

Of course today in the modern-day Canadian economy, when we speak of money we mean coins, currency, and other deposits; however, in our past, different articles have served as money. For example, in our early pre-Confederation history, fur trappers used playing cards during the winter to fulfill the functions of money, until the supply ships arrived in the spring with coins.

4) How is the Bank of Canada rate set?

The Bank of Canada determines a 50 basis point range over which the overnight lending rate can move up or down, and the Bank rate is set at the upper end of this range. These upper and lower limits are effectively a bid / ask spread at which the Bank will borrow funds from financial institutions or lend funds to investment dealers. This arrangement ensures that the overnight range stays within the operating band. When the operating band changes, this sends a clear signal to market participants about the direction of short-term interest rates that the Bank of Canada currently endorses.

CHAPTER 6

Managing Investments: Drawing it All Together

The key to early retirement or to retiring comfortably can be found by answering 3 essential questions:

(1) How much capital has been saved?

(2) How much investment income will the savings or capital generate?

(3) How much income does the retiree require in order to live comfortably?

Savings

Why should an individual save? There are a number of reasons why individuals should save on their own, without relying exclusively on government or employer-sponsored pension plans:

- To increase future consumption.
- To maintain current consumption if earnings fall.
- To stabilize consumption over a lifetime.
- To preserve a reasonable lifestyle.
- To build an estate for heirs.

Savings consist of spreading consumption over time; and they result from the postponement of current consumption in order to be able to fund future consumption. Consumption at some point in the future is determined by future savings, current savings already accumulated, and the investment return on the current savings (including the effects of income tax). Savings increase future purchasing power only if the real return on savings is positive, i.e. greater than the rate of inflation. Current savings, which are also called asset reserves, would include forced savings such as the Canada Pension Plan (CPP) and employer sponsored registered pension plans (RPPs). These types of forced savings plans affect the level of voluntary savings, but they will eventually contribute to future consumption.

The steps to building an investment portfolio

The purpose of an investment policy is to outline or provide a basis for an asset allocation mix that is suitable to the investor's goals, constraints, and risk tolerance. An investment policy establishes objectives along with the approach that is to be used to obtain them. The benefit of a written investment policy statement is to maximize the investor's well being and net worth while considering the financial objectives and any specific constraints that are imposed by the investor.

An investment policy must be formulated and based upon the specific circumstances and characteristics of each investor. These situation specific characteristics include:

- age,
- investment risk tolerance,
- capital currently available to invest,
- current income,
- the future need for investment capital and income, and
- the amount that is required to be saved on an ongoing basis.

The investment policy must take into account inflation, economic growth, and the investor's investment time horizon.

Additionally, an investment policy must consider the investor's consumption or desired consumption profile, which is influenced by 5 factors:

- Initial savings or wealth.
- Periodic income.
- Periodic savings.
- Real return generated on the portfolio.
- Consumption preferences i.e. the importance to the individual of trading off current consumption for the ability to consume in the future.

Establishing investment objectives

Typical investment objectives that must be considered and formulated into an investor's investment policy and asset allocation decisions include:

- Preservation of capital.
- Requirement for current investment income.
- Capital growth.
- Minimization of income taxes.
- Liquidity of the investment.

Introduction to portfolio management

In order to formulate a portfolio management strategy, it is important to understand some basic information regarding investing and investments.

Aninvestment is defined as any asset into which funds can be placed with the expectation that the invested capital will generate additional positive income; and many investors, will insist that, as a minimum requirement, the investment will preserve its value.

Many types of investments are available, ranging from those which will protect and retain capital, to the more aggressive derivative securities. Investors select investments to meet personal income goals and requirements, including interest income, capital growth, dividend income, and rental income.

Today, investors search beyond local markets for higher returns and foreign market diversification opportunities. Diversification plays an important role in lowering risk through the development of a portfolio that includes a number of different asset classes.

There are four steps in investment portfolio management:

(1) Identify investment objectives, preferences, and constraints and determine the resulting investment policy that is then documented.

(2) Determine and apply an investment strategy through the choice of specific financial and real assets, using the guidance of the investment policy statement.

(3) Monitor changes in market conditions and the circumstances of the specific investor.

(4) Adjust the portfolio to take into account any changes that occur.

Portfolio Management and Asset Allocation

Asset allocation is an important part of portfolio management. Asset allocation is the decision making process relating to the determination of:

- which asset classes are to be considered for inclusion in the investment portfolio,
- the proportion of funds which are to be allocated to each asset class, and
- the determination of how much money is to be invested into each security within individual asset classes.

There are three steps in the asset allocation process, which are undertaken by asset managers:

(1) Determine the financial and investment objectives. Investment strategy will differ according to the various personal objectives of investors. When the investor is seeking to maximize the total return on a portfolio, research has shown that it is more important to choose the right asset mix rather than the right investment within the asset class.

(2) Identify the investment constraints that are specific to the individual investor. Factors to be considered here are personal data such as:

- age,
- family obligations,
- income tax considerations,
- net worth,
- current income,
- investment personality, knowledge, temperament, risk tolerance, unacceptable risks,
- time horizon, and
- any other relevant investment constraints.

(3) Determine the allocation strategy. This step involves choosing a risk and reward combination which provides the highest levels of investor utility or satisfaction with which to achieve the financial objectives, while considering an investor's specific constraints and personal circumstances.

However, before developing an investment strategy it is necessary to determine whether or not the goals and objectives are realistic. It is important to comprehend all of the risks that are specific to each of the various components of the portfolio. This is critical in order to understand the relationship that exists between risk and the investment time horizon. It is also necessary to consider the benefits of a diversified portfolio.

Diversification

Diversification is a critical aspect of portfolio management, which can be achieved through asset allocation. An asset allocation program can:

- Diversify by asset class, which is usually expressed as a range of recommended percentages with a specified minimum and maximum limit.
- Diversify within asset classes.
- Diversify geographically.
- Review and re-balance the portfolio.

Diversification is a risk management technique that attempts to provide some insurance against the unexpected. The rule of thumb for diversification is to combine investments that have low or negative correlations, in order to eliminate specific and unique investment risk in a portfolio, until only market risk remains. When only market risk remains in a portfolio, options and futures derivative contracts can be used to hedge these risks.

Diversification also has an effect upon portfolio return; it reduces risk but it can also reduce a portfolio's maximum return. Diversification lessens the pressure to sell a particular holding and therefore, increases trading flexibility by extending the investor's time horizon.

Using a strategic approach to portfolio management, there are potentially three levels of diversification within an asset allocation model, and an investor should determine the answers to the following questions:

(1) How should the portfolio be apportioned between asset classes? Diversify between asset classes such as cash, fixed income, real estate, and equities.

(2) How should the portfolio be divided within each asset class? Diversify within each asset class by dividing the capital between conservative, moderate, or aggressive investments.

(3) What percentage of the portfolio should be invested outside of Canada? Diversify geographically to acquire the benefits of international diversity.

Risk and return in modern portfolio theory

For many investors, risk is generally considered to be related to bad news. What many individuals fail to realize is that all investment entails risk, and that any investor who wishes to obtain a return that is higher than the risk free rate must assume investment risk.

Modern portfolio theory is based on the premise that investors are rational beings who are risk averse and that given equal returns, will prefer an investment that has the lower risk. If 2 investments have equal risk, a rational investor will prefer the investment with a higher return. Investors are not as averse to risk as they are averse to losses.

A forecast of a security's return is an expected or anticipated value, which is representative of the investor's expectations of the return distribution for the security, and the expected return includes both the expected realized and unrealized annual income. Research studies confirm that historic returns are not good predictors of future returns.

The expected return of a portfolio is the weighted average of the expected returns of the individual securities that comprise it. However, the risk of a portfolio is a function of three factors:

- the relative weights of each of the assets which comprise the portfolio,
- the volatility of each of the portfolio's components as measured by the standard deviation of returns, and
- the correlation of the returns between each pair of assets which comprise the portfolio.

Analysts and academics use several tools to facilitate the evaluation of portfolios, one being the normality assumption. The normality assumption indicates that the returns on a security are clustered around a single number. Statisticians call this the central tendency towards the mean or average. This normality assumption allows an investor or portfolio manager to make selections of securities based on only 2 criteria: the expected return of the security, and the standard deviation of the security's return.

Standard deviation is a measure of the expected deviation or variability of returns in relation to the expected return. Standard deviation is a statistical measure of the spread of the security's returns. As a general rule, the higher the standard deviation, the higher the total risk of a security or a portfolio.

A portfolio's standard deviation can be calculated from the standard deviations of the individual securities that make up the portfolio. However, unlike the expected return, which is simply a weighted average, the standard deviation of a portfolio is always less than or equal to the weighted average of the standard deviations of the component securities. Furthermore, if the return distributions of the individual securities within a portfolio are not normally distributed, as the total number of securities held in the portfolio increases, the distribution of the portfolio's return tends towards normality.

The standard deviation associated with the return on an asset decreases with the square root of time. Therefore, the longer the investment horizon is, the lower the standard deviation of the annualized returns over the horizon will be. In other words, extending the time horizon decreases the risk of a stock investment in relation to a riskless asset. A minor forecasting mistake can have an important impact on the final portfolio value if the analysis horizon is long. For example, assume that an investment has an expected annual return of 10% with a standard deviation of ± 20%. This means that the return on the investment can vary from -10% to 30% in any given year. However, if the investment is held for 10 years, the standard deviation drops to ± 6.32%; after 25 years, the standard deviation is ± 4.0%; and after 45 years, the standard deviation drops to ± 3.98%. These calculations can be verified by using the following mathematical equation:

The Relationship between Investment Horizon and Risk

$$\sigma_{\bar{R}n} = \frac{\sigma_{R1}}{\sqrt{n}}$$

Where:

$\sigma_{\bar{R}n}$ = standard deviation of average return over n years

σ_{R1} = standard deviation of rate of return in 1 year

n = time in years

Another important measure used in portfolio analysis is correlation. Correlation describes how well 2 assets move relative to one another. The correlation coefficient describes the pattern of 2 asset's returns relative to one another. A correlation coefficient can range between -1.0 and +1.0. Assets are said to be perfectly positively correlated if the correlation coefficient equals 1.0 and the assets are said to be perfectly negatively correlated, if the correlation coefficient is -1.0. A correlation coefficient of 0.0 indicates that the returns of 2 assets are uncorrelated. In portfolio management, the intent is to locate and combine assets with low or negative correlations. For diversification purposes, a perfectly negative correlation is most attractive, since this indicates that the securities vary in opposite directions and fluctuations will tend to cancel one other. Correlation of -1.0 (perfect negative correlation) allows the risk of the portfolio as measured by the standard deviation to equal zero.

In the real investment world, there are no assets with perfectly negative correlation. However, one of the major reasons cited for the inclusion of foreign equities in a balanced portfolio, is the negative correlation between

North American and other stock markets. Furthermore, research also indicates that there is a negative correlation between equity markets and commercial real estate.

Methods for understanding and measuring risk tolerance

There is no unique, riskless asset, since all investments carry a risk of some type. However, by convention or proxy, federal government securities are considered risk free. For many years T-bills were considered the appropriate risk free investment against which to measure investment performance. However, the more sophisticated analysis that is supported by modern portfolio theory (MPT) suggests that better investment decisions can be reached when one assumes that there is one riskless asset for each selected investment horizon. For example, an investor with a 20 year time horizon would use a 20 year government of Canada bond as the appropriate risk free asset against which to measure portfolio returns.

The following concepts and techniques assist in gaining a better understanding of an individual's perceptions of investment risk as a whole. This knowledge is then used by the investor when determining the individual components that will eventually comprise a portfolio.

1. **Demographics.**
    - Men will usually accept higher risks than women will.
    - Risk tolerance decreases with age.
    - Risk tolerance increases with wealth, income, and education.
2. **Life-cycle approach.**
    - The accumulation phase is represented by a young person just starting out in a career. Priorities are usually to build up some savings, obtain life insurance, buy a home, and start a family. With a long investment time horizon, large risks can, theoretically, be taken.
    - In the middle years, an individual is in a position to start a serious savings program. Discretionary income is generally high and typically, a primary goal is retirement saving. The time horizon is generally still long, although income tax considerations are probably more important than in the accumulation phase. There is usually little need for current income, and the appropriate investment policy is generally one of real growth.

- At the time of retirement, there is usually a need for stable income and risk tolerance diminishes. Inflation protection may be desirable, and typically, the need for investment marketability is higher than in the other life-cycle stages.

3. **Investment personality or psychographics.**

   - Passive investors are inclined to be people who have acquired wealth passively for example by inheritance. Generally, these individuals have low-risk tolerance. Passive investors tend to be risk adverse trend followers, who prefer a well-diversified portfolio. Academic research shows that a large percentage of low and middle income families tend to produce passive investors.
   - Active investors on the other hand, tend to have a higher risk tolerance. These individuals typically, want to take control of their financial destiny. Active investors tend to be individuals who have earned their own wealth for example, entrepreneurs. Active investors typically follow a focused rather than a diversified investment policy. As well, active investors often have been raised in middle to upper income families.

Portfolio rebalancing

In managing a portfolio of investments, an investor will undertake changes in the portfolio from time to time due to a:

- Change in the specific circumstances of an individual investor.
- Change in the expected return of an asset.
- Change in the risk of an asset.
- Change in the correlation between 2 assets.
- Change in the risk free rate of return.
- Change in general economic conditions.

Asset mix techniques and rebalancing

The rebalancing of a portfolio involves both time, and transaction costs. Therefore, portfolios should be reviewed regularly for changes in material events in the individual investor's personal circumstances; and the relative appeal of the various portfolio components as market conditions evolve. Typically, asset mix decisions are made for one year at a time.

The most commonly encountered asset allocation techniques are strategic and tactical asset allocation.

- Strategic asset allocation is based on data covering the individual's investment horizon and dictates which asset groups should be emphasized or underweighted in the portfolio. The higher that an individual's aversion to risk is, the smaller the allowed deviations from the strategic allocation should be.
- Tactical asset allocation involves temporarily departing from the strategic weighting's in order to benefit from temporary imbalances in the securities markets.

Portfolio performance appraisal

The success of the portfolio manager is measured by comparing the total return of the portfolio to comparable benchmark portfolios. The most common calculation is based upon total return divided by the average amount invested.

Investments: Making the Choices

In order to create a portfolio of assets, it is imperative that individuals acquire knowledge of some of the basics of investment theory. These include stock and bond valuation techniques, factors which affect and cause price movements of individual investments, industry life cycles and other criteria in the investment environment which affect investment performance and which will therefore, impact the final investment decisions.

Factors that affect the market price of stocks and bonds

Investor expectations concerning interest rate movements and future inflation often guide investment purchase decisions. Expectations of future inflation rates are built into the interest rates and for example, fixed-rate bonds offer no protection against unanticipated and sustained periods of high inflation. Conversely, a variable-rate bond may offer some inflation protection. Investor expectations of the future earnings and dividend payments of a common stock determine the market value, although the value of assets is also an important factor. A great company in a growth industry however, can still perform poorly if the company disappoints the consensus of analysts' earnings estimates. Large transactions may affect prices temporarily creating bid-ask imbalances. Stock prices can also be affected by rumours, or by public tender offers.

Stock valuation

Many tools exist that can be used to value equity securities. It is recommended that some form of analysis be performed before purchasing a corporation's stock. Company performance analysis usually includes a review of the historic trends. Although past performance is no indication of future performance, a reasonable assumption is that things will continue as they have in the past.

Fundamental analysis is the evaluation of a company based on its historic financial statements combined with an analysis of the company's future prospects.

Trend analysis would review historic sales, profits and debt levels. Trend analysis would also review valuation ratios such as the price earnings ratio (P/E), price to book value, book value per share, and price to sales.

Other corporate factors that are valuable when analysing company performance include the product line, product quality, human resource needs, training, and the technological state of machinery or equipment.

The valuation tools used most frequently by investors and analysts include:

1. The dividend discount model (DDM). This is a method for calculating the market price of a blue-chip company's common shares. The value of a common stock is the present value of all future dividend payments.

2. The price to earnings (P/E) ratio is calculated as the price of the common share divided by earnings per common share. A company with higher quality earnings should have a higher P/E ratio than a company with low quality earnings. A growth company will have a higher P/E ratio than a stable company. The P/E ratio for a company should be compared to other companies in the same industry. It is important to note that the P/E ratio is the inverse of market interest rates and when consumer confidence is high, P/E ratios will tend to be high.

3. Growth is not always a blessing. Without careful financial planning, growth can cause cash flow problems. A company's sustainable growth rate is the maximum rate at which it can grow without straining its financial resources. The long-term sustainable growth rate (g) is calculated as the product of the return on equity (ROE) and the company's earnings retention rate (RR). If the actual growth rate exceeds the sustainable growth rate, the company must eventu-

ally raise additional capital. To raise capital internally, a company can sell equity, increase financial leverage by issuing bonds, reduce dividends, sell marginal operations, outsource production or administration, or increase prices. Externally, a company can seek a merger partner or acquirer.

4. One powerful analytical tool to analyse a company's return on equity (ROE) is the DuPont method of analysis. There are a number of variations of the DuPont analytical technique, which break down the relationship between net income and shareholders equity. One method of ROE analysis uses 3 components that show the relationship of the firm's net profit margin, total asset turnover, and financial leverage. Another, more sophisticated method of ROE analysis uses 5 components that show the interaction of the operating profit margin, total asset turnover, interest expense rate, financial leverage multiplier and tax retention rate. These various components help investors to analyse the efficiency of a corporation's competitive situation, internal operations, the use of financial leverage, and the impact of the government tax policies.

Bond valuation

The price of a bond is based on its coupon, maturity and prevailing market interest rates. Bond price volatility depends upon the cash coupon and the time remaining until the bonds maturity.

The market value of a bond equals the present value of all future cash flows accruing to the investor. Cash flows for the conservative bond investor include periodic interest payments and principal return. Cash flows for the aggressive bond trader may include periodic interest payments and the capital gained or lost when the bond is sold before its maturity.

Bond price movements

Any investor contemplating the inclusion of bonds into a portfolio requires an understanding of how and when bond prices change in the marketplace. The coupon rate of the issue, the features of the issue, the credit rating of the issuer, and, the term to maturity can affect the bond's market price. The current level of interest rates determines bond prices in the secondary market. When interest rates rise, bond prices fall, on the other hand, when interest rates fall, bond prices rise. A bond's price therefore is said to vary inversely with market interest rates.

A bond with a high coupon rate will trade at a higher price and with less volatility than will a similar bond with a low coupon rate. The greater the portion of the yield that the investor receives through coupon payments (cash income) rather than through the value of the bond at maturity (capital gain), the smaller the risk and therefore, the higher and more stable, a bond's price. In other words, cash flow has value. Cash flow cushions the variability in price movement of the bond. Therefore, high coupon bonds are sometimes known as cushion bonds.

Features of a debt issue include convertibility, call provisions, sinking funds, and purchase funds, any and all of which can affect the market price of the bond. The higher the credit rating of the issuer, the higher the price of the bond, everything else equal. The closer a bond is to the maturity date, the smaller will be the variation from the par value of the bond.

During periods of rising interest rates, the prices of longer-term bonds usually decline more than the prices of shorter term bonds. When interest rates fall, however, prices of longer term bonds tend to rise the most. Longer term bonds are, therefore, more volatile than short term bonds. Lower coupon bonds are more volatile than high coupon bonds. Bond prices, in general, are more volatile when market interest rates are low.

The market price of a fixed income bond depends on its coupon, maturity date and the prevailing market interest rate. Prices decline when interest rates rise and bond prices rise when interest rates decline in order to adjust the price and to reflect a competitive yield. A change in the issuer's credit rating can also cause a fluctuation in price, as higher risk is reflected in the price/yield relationship. Even without a formal rating change, reduced demand can cause lower bond prices and higher yields. For example, this is rapidly reflected in the price of junk bonds when market participants fear that a recession will lead to an increase in defaults. Poor business conditions over a prolonged period can cause financial weakness and jeopardize the firm's ability to pay interest.

Purchasing a bond when interest rates are high is preferable, because the highest yields can be locked in for the long-term. Holding bonds is most attractive when rates are declining, due to the upward movement in the market prices of fixed income securities. Falling interest rate periods are boom times for bondholders.

Bond prices are quoted in daily newspapers and are easily available over the Internet.

Industry life cycles

The profitability of an industry tends to be a function of the competitive structure within the industry. The competitive structure, the amount, and the intensity of the competition within the industry are important because these factors determine the prices, costs, advertising, and the overall investment that a firm is required to make in order to compete successfully. The competitive environment in which a company operates can have a dramatic impact on its stock price. A company's long-term survival depends upon its ability to exploit its long-term sustainable competitive advantage. There are three generic competitive strategies that are used by a corporation's management in order to accomplish the firm's strategic objectives — cost leadership, differentiation, and focus.

- Cost leadership means that a firm sets out to become the low-cost producer in its industry.
- A firm implementing a differentiation strategy seeks to be unique, and the reward for that uniqueness is a premium price.
- The focus strategy has 2 variations. A **cost focus** seeks a cost advantage in the target segment, while a **differentiation focus** pursues differences within a target niche.

Industry analysis is the study of industry groupings including an examination of the competitive position of a particular industry in relation to other industries. The intent is to identify companies that show particular promise within an industry. These analyses are affected by demographic and social changes. An integral part of any industry analysis will be to determine the industry's stage in its growth cycle. Additionally, it is important to bear in mind that governments can impact an industry and its future prospects through regulations, deregulation, taxes and subsidies.

Like people, industries and companies tend to go through predictable stages. Understanding where an industry is located in its life-cycle will enable the investor to make better investment decisions, since different types of valuation methods are used for companies in different stages of maturity. Additionally, the stage of the life cycle has a tremendous impact upon business risk.

Stages or phases of the industry life cycle

1. The developmental or formative stage.
    - This stage is often driven by entrepreneurial and innovative focus.

- The industry sales and earnings are usually small or possibly negative.
- Growth prospects are high.
- Competition tends to increase during the progression of this phase as other entrepreneurs recognize the market potential.
- High risks exist in this stage since there is uncertainty as to whether or not consumers will widely accept the product, and which firms will survive.
- Venture capitalists are often active during this stage.

2. The expansion or growth stage.
   - This stage is characterized by rapid growth of both unit sales and profits.
   - Market leaders tend to emerge due to consolidation and shakeout of weak competitors.
   - Consumer acceptance broadens the market as the leaders improve the product.
   - Risk in this stage declines due to increased consumer acceptance and customer loyalty starts to build.
   - Companies start to go public with initial public offerings (IPO).
   - Companies are inclined to reinvest earnings therefore, little or no dividends are paid to investors, but return on equity (ROE) tends to be high.
3. The maturity stage.
   - This is usually the longest stage in the life cycle and can last for many decades.
   - Typically, in this stage, approximately 80% of the market has been saturated.
   - The growth rate slows and stabilizes at a level that is sustainable over a long period of time, due to competition and shrinking profit margins.
   - Firms often expand into additional market niches by developing add-ons for the original product, which helps to sustain a higher growth rate.

- As growth slows, the need to expand production facilities declines, which reduces the need for capital expenditures, improving the firm's overall financial flexibility.
- Excess cash that previously has been reinvested into expansion is now available to reduce corporate debt or to be paid as dividends to investors.

4. The declining or harvesting stage.
   - The real growth rate tends to decline to a level that is less than that of the overall economy.
   - Substitute products and technologies tend to make the industry's product obsolete.
   - Firms tend to focus on keeping costs down, in order to maintain, or slow the decline in profit margins and profits.
   - Firms may actually sell production assets that are no longer required.
   - Dividends paid to investors tend to be large.
   - The firms in this stage are often referred to as cash cows.
   - However, it is possible for firms and industries to perpetuate themselves by becoming more dynamic and by adding new products or new product lines.

Demographic and social changes

Demographic and social changes may have a dramatic influence on the outlook for an industry, or company. This, in turn, will affect investor expectations and therefore the market price of the firm's securities.

- **Age distribution.** The baby boom generation, which was born between 1946 in 1963, has already and will continue to have a dramatic impact on the relative fortunes of industries and firms. As baby boomers continue to grow older, they will increase the demand for health-care services, pharmaceuticals, retirement communities, and other leisure activities such as RV's, travel, and cruises.
- **Income distribution.** As baby boomers reach the ages of 45-54 which is typically when family incomes are at their highest, demand for luxury goods should also rise. Diversity in income distribution should lead to more niche markets. Companies that do not target but

instead employ a shotgun approach to marketing may find the demand for their products shrinking.

- **Distribution of the industrial mix.** The shift away from the traditional Canadian resource industries and towards service and technology, which require a highly skilled workforce, can affect the future prospects of firms.

International considerations

The changes in flows of exported goods and services have a dramatic impact on the Canadian domestic economy because capital flows influence both interest rates and exchange rates. An investor must be cognizant of the political and economic prospects for our major trading partners and recognize the effects these factors will have on Canadian companies.

Interest rates

Monetary and fiscal policy can affect domestic interest rates.

An inversion of the yield curve occurs when short-term interest rates are higher than long-term interest rates. This often signals a decline in the near future for the stock markets, as investors seeking the safety of high yielding, short-term treasury bills, abandon equities.

A decline in long-term interest rates usually results in higher stock prices since there is greater demand for stocks and less demand for long-term bonds.

Glossary

Abnormal return. The return on a security that is different from that which is expected based on its risk profile.

Accounts Payable. Money which is owed to a supplier.

Accounts Receivable. Money which is owed by a customer.

Accrual accounting. Method of accounting the shows revenue and expenses in a specific period whether or not cash has actually changed hands.

Asset allocation. The process of apportioning an investor's wealth between different asset classes for investment purposes.

Asset mix. The process of distributing assets in a portfolio among various asset classes to optimize the investor's risk / reward trade off.

Auction market. Securities market at a fixed location, where prices are determined by buyers and sellers.

Autocorrelation test. Test of the efficient market hypothesis (EMH) to determine if there are predictable correlation patterns in a security's price over time.

Balance sheet. A financial statement that quantifies assets, liabilities, and net equity as of a specific date.

Benchmark error. Descriptive term for the situation in which an improper or inaccurate standard is used to assess the performance of an investment portfolio and its management.

Benchmark portfolio. A benchmark portfolio is used to evaluate the investment performance of the portfolio manager.

Beta. A quantitative, standardized, measure of a security's systematic risk based upon the asset's covariance or volatility, with the market portfolio. A security with a Beta of 1.0 exactly matches the variability of the market portfolio.

Blue chip. A significant, known and well-managed common stock. Blue-chip stocks typically have strong investment qualities such as a record of consistent profitability with a history of continuous and growing dividend payments.

Business risk. The degree of uncertainty of income and cash flows caused by doing business in a particular industry.

Capital asset pricing model (CAPM). An economic valuation model that derives the expected rate of return of an asset based on that asset's systematic risk level.

Capital market line (CML). The trade-off between risk and return for efficient portfolios.

Capital market theory. Describes how assets are priced in the marketplace.

Characteristic line. The line of best fit which results from the regression of the return on a stock or mutual fund on the market return. The slope of the characteristic line indicates the security's market risk.

Charting. Descriptive term for the classic technical analytical technique of graphing price and volume in order to detect patterns in the price movement.

Coefficient of determination. The square of the correlation coefficient. Measures the percentage of the variance in the dependent variable that is explained by the independent variable.

Coefficient of variation (CV). Statistical measure of the variability relative to return and it indicates the risk per unit of return. Calculated as standard deviation divided by expected return.

Completely diversified portfolio. Descriptive term for a portfolio in which diversification has eliminated all specific non-market risk.

Composite (risk adjusted). Measures of portfolio performance that combine risk and return into a single calculation or estimate.

Constant ratio plan. A portfolio management strategy by which the investor's strategic asset allocation mix is maintained through periodic adjustments. For example, an investor with $50,000 and with an 80%--20% formula might start with $40,000 in stocks and $10,000 in fixed income. If the stock portion of the portfolio increased in value to $50,000 and the fixed income assets remained unchanged, the investor would restore the constant ratio by selling $2,000 of stock and buying an additional $2,000 of bonds or other fixed income securities.

Contrarian. One who trades or invests in a manner which is opposite to that of the crowd.

Correlation coefficient. Statistical measure used to quantify the degree to which the movements of 2 assets are related to one another. The correlation coefficient ranges between -1.00 and +1.00.

Covariance. An absolute statistical measure of the degree to which the returns on 2 securities tend to be related to one other.

Cyclical company. A firm whose earnings rise and fall with the economy, e.g., a mining company.

Defensive company. A firm whose future earnings are likely to withstand an economic downturn.

Defensive stock. A stock whose return investors do not expect to decline as much as the overall market during a downturn or bear market. The stock of a company with a record of high-quality earnings and continuous dividend payments, which has shown relative stability in poor economic conditions, e.g. a utility company.

Diffusion index. Indicates the number of stocks rising in price relative to the number of stocks declining or which are unchanged in price, during a specified time frame.

Dividend discount model (DDM). A valuation technique used for estimating the intrinsic value of a stock. DDM models calculate the discounted present value of all future dividends. DDMs describe the relationship between a stock's current price and the present value of all future dividend payments or earnings.

Dividend reinvestment plan (DRIP). Plan offered by a company that allows stockholders to reinvest dividends in additional shares of stock at no cost.

Dollar weighted rate of return. Portfolio performance measurement method which is affected by the cash inflows and outflows over which the portfolio manager has no control. It is the portfolio's internal rate of return (IRR).

Dow theory. The oldest theory of technical analysis. The Dow theory is based on primary, secondary, and daily price movements of the stocks which comprise the Dow Jones industrial average.

EAFE index. An index of foreign equity market performance. Composed of major markets located in Europe, Australia, and the Far East.

Earnings Statement or Income Statement or the Profit and Loss Statement or the Statement of Revenue and Expenses or the P&L. A financial statement that details the results of a company's net operational profits or losses over a period.

Earnings surprise. The difference between expected and actual earnings for a firm.

Efficient capital market. A market in which a security's price rapidly reflects all information about the security.

Efficient frontier. The set of portfolios which have the maximum expected return for a given level of risk. Alternatively, the efficient frontier can also represent portfolios that have the minimum risk for a given expected return.

Efficient market hypothesis (EMH). Theory which asserts that securities markets are efficient and that the prices of securities reflect their true economic value.

Efficient portfolio. A portfolio that has the greatest expected return for a given risk level or alternatively, the least risk for a given expected return.

Ex ante. Term used to describe forward looking, anticipated, or predicted returns.

Excess return. The return on a security which is above that of the overall market.

Expected return. The anticipated, or mean weighted average, of all of the possible returns of a probability distribution, given the probable outcomes from an investment. A hypothetical value.

Ex post. The term used to describe backward looking, historic, or actual returns.

Fisher theory. Asserts that the nominal risk-free interest rate is equal to the real rate of interest plus an inflation premium.

Fixed asset. A balance sheet item. Tangible, long-term assets that are held for use by the business and used to earn revenue. Examples are real estate or equipment.

Formula investing. An investment strategy based on buying or selling an investment at a pre-specified or predetermined price or asset allocation weighting. The purpose of formula investing is to eliminate emotion from the investment management process. For example, formula investing might call for the shifting of funds from common shares to fixed income as the stock market rises above a certain predetermined point, or the reallocation of funds to common share investments as the stock market average declines.

Full replication. A passive index which is constructed by purchasing securities in proportion to their weight within the index.

Fundamental analysis. Fundamental analysis considers a corporation's financial information and the economic factors, which affect the company's business.

Geometric mean. Describes the true average compounded return over multiple periods. Accurate measure of the realized change in wealth over multiple time frames. The geometric mean will always be less than the arithmetic mean. Calculated as the nth root of the product of the annual holding period returns over n years minus 1.0.

Growth company. Company that consistently invests in projects that provide rates of returns that exceed the firm's cost of capital. Because of these investment opportunities, a growth company retains most of its earnings.

Hedgers. Investors who minimize the risk of financial loss by making counterbalancing arrangements.

Indexing. A passive portfolio management strategy intended to match the composition and performance of a selected benchmark or index.

Indifference curve. A graphic representation which describes an investor's preferences or aversion between risk and return.

Initial public offering (IPO). The sale of stock that has no existing public market.

Intangible asset. An asset with no physical form, e.g., goodwill.

Internal growth rate (g). Calculated as ROE times earnings retention rate. Describes the maximum growth rate for a firm without the use of outside financing.

Investment horizon. A descriptive term for the time frame used for investment planning and forecasting purposes. Also refers to the point in the future at which the investor requires the return of the invested funds.

Liabilities. The financial debts or obligations of a company. Liabilities are a balance sheet category and are usually divided into current liabilities (payable within one year) and long-term liabilities (payable after one year).

Market average. An arithmetic mean of the prices of securities.

Market model. A linear relationship that relates the return on a security to the return on the market.

Market portfolio. Theoretical portfolio which is composed of all risky assets. Each asset is weighted in the portfolio by the ratio of its market value to the market value of all risky assets. In the CAPM model, it represents the optimum portfolio of risky assets for all investors.

Market risk premium. The return above the risk-free rate that investors demand as compensation for accepting systematic risk.

Mean. Simple arithmetic average.

Mean rate of return. The average of a security's return which is measured over an extended time frame.

Median. The middle number in a population or distribution.

Mode. The value that occurs most frequently in a distribution.

Modern portfolio theory (MPT). A sophisticated tool for investment decision making that estimates, and controls both the risk and expected return of a combination of investments.

Net return. Yield or return calculated after income taxes.

Non-systematic risk. Descriptive term for diversifiable risk, which is unique and specific to the security.

Odd lot theory. Asserts that small investors often trade less than 100 shares and that these unsophisticated investors usually make incorrect investment decisions.

Overbought. Descriptive term for the market condition which implies that the market or security has risen too quickly and is susceptible to a correction.

Oversold. Descriptive term for market conditions. Oversold implies that the market or security is depressed in price relative to historical levels.

Overweighted. Descriptive term for a portfolio that includes more of a specific security than if based on market value alone.

Payout ratio. Dividends divided by earnings.

Performance attribution. Seeks to identify why a particular portfolio was successful or not.

Performance measurement. The relevant area of Modern portfolio theory (MPT) that attempts to measure the risk adjusted return.

Policy statement. A written expression of an investor's investment goals, constraints, and risk tolerance.

Portfolio. A group of investments owned by the same investor. Ideally, the investments should have different patterns or correlations of returns over time, in order to reduce investment risks.

Portfolio optimization. The process of determining the portfolio with the highest return and minimum risk.

Price/earning (P/E ratio) or earnings multiplier. A valuation measure. The number by which earnings per share is multiplied to estimate a stock's value. Calculated as the common stock's current market price divided by its expected per share earnings.

Quantitative analysis. The method of stock valuation that studies the numerical, measurable, characteristics to search for undervalued anomalies.

Retention rate (RR). 1.0 minus the dividend payout ratio.

Risk. Exposure to uncertainty. The probability that an investment's actual return will deviate or vary from its expected return.

Risk averse. A descriptive term for a rational and conservative investor who is unwilling to accept the probability or chance of losing capital without adequate compensation.

Risk-free asset. An asset with an expected rate of return, and a standard deviation of zero. This hypothetical asset is non-existent however, it is in practice typically assumed to be a noncallable, default free federal government debt security.

Risk-free return. The return on a risk-free asset, that is earned with perfect certainty. This hypothetical return is usually proxied by federal government securities.

Risk premium. The additional return that is demanded by rational investors, in excess of the risk-free return, as compensation for assuming the additional risk of the uncertainty of an investment's return.

Risk tolerant. A term used to describe an investor who is both willing and able to accept the possibility of declining capital.

R squared. The percentage of a portfolio's return that can be explained by its beta or market risk.

Security market line (SML). Graphic representation of the capital asset pricing model (CAPM).

Sharpe measure. Portfolio management performance appraisal method that measures the portfolio's return vs. total risk. Calculated as portfolio return less the risk-free rate divided by the portfolio standard deviation.

Standard deviation. Statistical measure used to quantify the variability or dispersion of an asset's distribution of returns about the average or mean. In modern portfolio theory, standard deviation is a measure of total risk.

Statement of Changes in Financial Position. A financial statement that provides annual, corporate cash flow information. Cash flow statements are used to evaluate the company's continuing ability to generate cash internally, repay debts, reinvest and pay dividends to shareholders.

Sustainable growth rate (g). A measure of how quickly a firm can grow using internal equity and debt financing to keep the capital structure constant over time.

Systematic (non-diversifiable) risk. That part of risk which cannot be diversified away. This risk influences a large number of assets and therefore, is also called market risk. In modern portfolio theory beta is used to measure this portion of total risk.

Technical analysis. Estimation of future security price movements based on past price and volume movements.

Time weighted rate of return. Measures the actual performance of a portfolio manager and is not affected by cash flows.

Trading rule. A formula for deciding current transactions based on historical data.

Treynor measure. Portfolio management performance appraisal method that measures the portfolio's return vs. market risk. Calculated as portfolio return less the risk-free rate divided by the beta of the portfolio.

Total risk. The sum of an investment's non-diversifiable and diversifiable risks.

Underweighted. Descriptive term for a portfolio that includes less of a security than if the weighting was based on market value alone.

Unsystematic (diversifiable) risk. That part of risk that is non-market related and it is specific or unique to an individual company or asset. Unsystematic risk can be virtually eliminated through portfolio diversification.

Valuation process. Part of the investment decision process in which an estimate is made of the value of a company, security, or other asset.

Variance. A measure of variability. Variance measures the dispersion or deviation of outcomes. Standard deviation is the square root of variance.

Volatility. Describes the fluctuations in the price of a security. The sensitivity of a stock relative to changes in the market is traditionally measured by the beta of the security.

Wealth. Present value of all future income.

Questions

1) How does an investor calculate a corporation's cash flow from the financial statements?

Cash flow can be approximated from the Income Statement (one of the required financial statements included in a corporation's annual report). It can be calculated by taking net income before extraordinary items plus depreciation or amortization or depletion, plus the increase in deferred income taxes, plus minority interest, minus equity income.

2) How should an investor analyze bonds?

Analysis of the financial statements provides a simple method of judging the quality of most investments, including bonds. Financial statement analysis looks at relationships between Balance Sheet and Income Statement accounts. Some classic ratios for analyzing bond investments from information which can be found in the financial statements are: the debt to equity ratio, the times interest-earned ratio and the asset coverage ratio.

3) How would an investor know if bonds or equities were the best investment for their portfolio?

In order to answer this question it is important to understand the individual's investment risk tolerance, investment time horizon, knowledge level, net worth, age, and investment income needs. A mixture of bonds and equities may be appropriate for many individuals portfolios. However, generally speaking an investor at age 65, with a 10-year investment horizon and a medium risk tolerance will hold within the portfolio a larger component of bonds than a younger person with an investment horizon of 30 years. Additionally, for those requiring income, bonds or dividend paying stock's are more appropriate as compared to growth oriented common shares. Financial advisors would recommend that a complete investment profile be completed to determine the mix of bonds of vs. stocks that should be included in the individual's portfolio.

4) What are the tax consequences of investing in bonds or equities?

Bonds

When held outside of a tax-deferred savings vehicle, the interest earned on a marketable government bond is fully taxable.

Government bonds usually carry coupon interest, with interest normally paid semi-annually. Bondholders include in their taxable income the interest income when paid, or when it becomes receivable. Even if bondholders do not receive interest, such as a person owning a zero-coupon bond, they must accrue and include it annually in income according to the *Income Tax Act.*

Bonds sold before maturity will also be subject to capital gains or losses.

Government obligations are very popular securities for tax-deferred retirement accounts like RRSPs and RRIFs. These investments are held within a registered retirement savings plan (RRSP) or within a registered retirement income fund (RRIF), therefore all the growth of the investment is deferred. Taxes are eventually paid when these funds are drawn from the retirement savings vehicle. All withdrawals from a registered savings vehicle are taxable as ordinary income.

A bond held outside of a registered plan will earn interest that is taxed as ordinary income at the individual taxpayers marginal tax rate (MTR). Bonds that are sold before maturity may earn either capital gains or capital losses depending upon the difference in the price at which the bond was originally purchased and the price at which the bond is eventually sold. 3/4 or 75% of capital gains are included in income and are taxable to a Canadian.

Dividend income

If a stock produces dividends, these dividends will also be taxed. The dividends of taxable Canadian corporations qualify for special tax treatment called the dividend tax credit (DTC). Dividends from taxable Canadian corporations (but not foreign corporations) are subject to less personal income tax than are interest, or capital gains. Accordingly, a shift of investments into dividend paying Canadian stocks can reduce taxes and improve after-tax yields.

The federal dividend tax credit (DTC) makes the purchase of dividend paying shares of taxable Canadian companies particularly attractive to individual Canadians. The dividend tax credit system has been designed to provide a credit to shareholders for all or part of the tax already paid by the corporation on its earnings before the dividend was declared and distributed. There is no similar credit for interest paid by a corporation because a corporation, for income tax purposes, can deduct the interest cost from revenues earned. Comparing the after-tax yield on potential investments to make an appropriate investment decision is always important. The effect of the dividend tax credit is such that an interest-bearing investment needs to yield about 25% more than a comparable dividend yield (assuming all other factors such as risk, liquidity and so on are equal) in order for investors to retain the same net, after-tax income.

With respect to the preferential tax treatment received on dividend income from taxable Canadian corporations, the taxpayer is required to gross up the amount of the dividend by 25%. For example, if an individual received a $160 dividend, it would be reported for tax purposes as $200 of taxable income. Taxpayers then claim a credit of 13.33% of the grossed up amount or $26.67, and this credit reduces federal income taxes payable.

Dividends received from foreign companies are treated and taxed as ordinary taxable income but with the additional benefit of claiming a foreign tax credit.

Established companies are more likely to pay dividends regularly than are growth firms that tend to reinvest their earnings. Regular dividends suggest to investors that payments will be maintained, barring a major reduction in earnings. Additional dividends called extra dividends, caution an investor that the extra portion is a bonus that may not be repeated in the future.

Some companies offer dividend reinvestment programs (DRIPs), where dividend payments are used to purchase additional shares rather than being paid out in cash. Such reinvested dividends are taxable, just as cash dividends are. The shareholder usually benefits because they do not pay commissions to acquire these additional shares. Additionally, there is no premium paid for odd lot purchases when purchasing through a dividend reinvestment plan (DRIP).

Some companies declare stock dividends. This occurs when additional shares are issued as a dividend rather than paying a dividend in cash. By issuing a stock dividend a company still pays a dividend but conserves cash. For tax purposes, a stock dividend is treated the same as a regular cash dividend.

Holding a Canadian company's preferred stock within a tax deferral vehicle would not be advisable. The preferential tax treatment of the dividend tax credit is lost within the shelter of the tax-deferred vehicle. It is more tax efficient to shelter interest-bearing investments within a tax-deferred vehicle, and to hold preferentially taxed capital gains and dividend producing securities outside these tax shelters.

Capital gains

Gains on the sale of stock receive preferential capital gains treatment, specifically, 75% of capital gains are taxable at the investor's marginal tax rate. For income tax purposes Canadians may only deduct capital losses from capital gains.

Common stocks are usually purchased for capital appreciation. However, investors can purchase common stocks for income especially if the investor's goals also include some capital appreciation. Stocks are most attractive as holdings when interest rates are low; business conditions are stable, and when economic conditions generally favour slow and steady long-term growth of earnings and profits.

Some companies split their stock. This technique is used to bring a high-priced stock into a more popular market price range. A stock split broadens the distribution of a company's shares, and therefore increases the marketability of these shares. A stock split is described in terms of a ratio. For each 100 shares, priced at $9/share that splits three for one, the investor receives an additional 200 shares for a total of 300 shares owned, and priced at $3/share. The total dollar value of the account remains unchanged at $900.

Historically, over the long term, stocks have risen in value and increased dividends with inflation.

5) How should an investor go about building an investment portfolio?

An investor should first decide on their goals, which will be used to establish documented investment objectives, including a risk tolerance assessment. The next step is to set the asset allocation amongst the various asset classes, which maximizes the portfolio return while minimizing the investor's risk. Once the portfolio is assembled, it must be regularly reviewed and monitored to ensure that the portfolio continues to meet the investor's changing needs.

6) What techniques are available to an investor for allocating funds amongst asset classes?

One can use strategic asset allocation, a passive portfolio management technique, which sets the long-term mix for a particular investor. Tactical asset allocation is an active management technique that allows for discretionary and opportunistic deviations from the long-term strategic allocation. Dynamic allocation, an active investment management technique, permits a great deal of discretion and allows the investor to pursue the most profitable opportunities. An integrated asset allocation approach can include all of the above methods.

7) Why should real estate be part of a portfolio?

Research studies show that real estate offers a long term, attractive real rate of return and acts as a hedge to inflation. Commercial real estate has a lower standard deviation of return (risk) as compared to stocks or bonds. What is most important, is that the returns on real estate investments exhibit negative correlation with the other asset classes, which results in improved diversification when real estate is included as an asset class in a portfolio.

8) How does one know if a mutual fund manager is doing a good job?

Research indicates that only about one third of mutual fund managers outperform the benchmark portfolio after factoring in expenses and risk. This same research also concludes that mutual fund performance is inconsistent, which means that a top-performing fund in one year is seldom the top performer in the following year. Studies indicate that although professional money managers can outperform the index, the costs to find these opportunities can most often be greater than the additional returns.

9) What are the benefits of international diversification?

Investing globally means that an investor has more investment options to choose from and therefore, one benefit of international investment is the potential for higher returns. Another benefit of international investing is that the correlation of returns between domestic and foreign investments is low and diversification is best achieved by combining assets with negative or low correlations. Combining assets that are highly correlated does not reduce risk. Warning! The research suggests that global diversification must be done carefully, considering regional factors. For example, the Canadian stock markets are highly correlated to the U.S. markets, which means that combining U.S. stocks and Canadian stocks results in a minimal reduction of risk, unless a very careful analysis is performed.

10) How can standard deviation be used to evaluate the risk of a stock or mutual fund?

Standard deviation is considered to be a measure of total risk. In general, the higher the standard deviation of an asset's returns, the greater the risk.

11) An investor is considering the purchase of a Province of Alberta bond with a 10% coupon rate and $1,000 par or maturity value. Interest is paid semi-annually, and the bond matures in 15 years. If an investor requires an 8% rate of return, what is the maximum price that the investor would pay today?

The current market price of a bond is the sum of the present value (PV) of the coupon interest stream plus the present value (PV) of the face value, discounted at the investors required rate of return.

This problem is easily solved using a financial calculator. The key strokes are as follows:

Since the bond assumes semi-annual compounding, we must adjust the discount rate (i), the coupon interest payment (pmt), and the number of compounding periods (n) appropriately.

$n = 15 \text{ years} \times 2 = 30$ semi-annual compounding periods

$i = 8\% / 2 = 4\%$ semi-annual periodic interest rate

$pmt = \$100 / 2 = \$50$ semi-annual periodic interest payment

compute PV.

PV = \$864.60

Mathematically this can be written as:

$$\text{Bond Price} = \sum_{t=1}^{2n} \frac{I/2}{(1 + k/2)^t} + \frac{M}{(1 + k/2)^{2n}}$$

where:

$I/2$ = dollar amount of each interest payment

n = number of years to maturity

k = required rate of return

M = par or maturity value of the bond

Appendix

The Mathematics of Portfolio Management

Essential symbols

w = weight, or proportion of the total

r = correlation coefficient

R = coefficient of determination

$\mathbf{E_R}$ = expected return

$\mathbf{k_M}$ = expected return on the market portfolio

$\mathbf{k_n}$ = expected return on the nth asset

$\mathbf{k_{RF}}$ = risk-free rate of return

B = beta, a measure of an asset's nondiversifible risk

σ = standard deviation

COV = covariance of an asset

CAPM = Capital Asset Pricing Model

ROE = Return on Equity

s = sample standard deviation

n = number of observations

Expected return on a portfolio composed of n Assets

$$\overline{E_R} = w_1\overline{k_1} + w_2\overline{k_2} + w_3\overline{k_3} + \dots + w_n\overline{k_n}$$

Risk for a 2 Asset Portfolio

$$\sigma_p^2 = w_1^2\sigma_p^2 + w_2^2\sigma_2^2 + 2w_1w_2r_{1,2}\sigma_1\sigma_2$$

Beta for investment i relative to the Market

$$\beta_i = \frac{COV_{i,M}}{\sigma_M^2} = \frac{\sigma_i\sigma_M r_{i,M}}{\sigma_M^2}$$

Correlation Coefficient for assets a and b

$$\text{correlation coefficient} = r_{a,b} = \frac{COV_{a,b}}{\sigma_a\sigma_b}$$

Sample Standard Deviation of Returns for n observations

$$s = \sqrt{\frac{\sum_{t=1}^{n}(k_t - \overline{k})^2}{n-1}}$$

Expected return on asset n according to the Capital Asset Pricing Model(CAPM)

$$\text{CAPM } E_R = k_{RF} + \beta_n (k_M - k_{RF})$$

Arithmetic Mean (simple average)

$$\overline{k} = \frac{1}{n}\sum_{t=1}^{n} k_t = \frac{\Sigma k}{n}$$

Geometric Mean (compound average)

$$\tilde{k} = [(1 + k_1) \times (1 + k_2) \times \dots \times (1 + k_n)]^{1/n} - 1$$

Holding Period Return

$$HPR = \frac{\text{Ending value of Investment}}{\text{Beginning Value of Investment}}$$

DuPont Analysis of Return on Equity

ROE = Profit Margin × Asset Turnover × Financial Leverage

$$ROE = \frac{\text{Net Income}}{\text{Equity}} = \frac{\text{Net Income}}{\text{Sales}} \times \frac{\text{Sales}}{\text{Assets}} \times \frac{\text{Assets}}{\text{Equity}}$$

Long Term Sustainable Growth Rate for a Firm

$g = ROE \times RR$

Retention Ratio of Earnings

RR = (1 – Dividend Payout Ratio)

Ratios Used to Analyze Financial Statements

Profitability

Return on Equity $\frac{\text{Net Income}}{\text{Closing Common Equity}}$

This ratio is used to determine the adequacy of the return on common shareholder's investment. Generally, the higher the ROE the better.

Return on Assets $\frac{\text{Net Income}}{\text{Total Assets}}$

This ratio measures the effectiveness to which management is employing the firm's resources. The ROA measures the return that the company earned on its assets; it does not measure the return earned by an investor. Low ROA might indicate poor management ability. Low ROA may also indicate that further analysis of the firm's assets might reveal inefficient assets which can be disposed of and converted to cash.

Operations

Gross Profit Margin $\frac{\text{Gross Profit}}{\text{Net Sales}}$

This ratio indicates the % of gross profit that is earned on each dollar of sales. The gross profit margin for a firm should be compared to the industry averages.

Net Profit Margin $\frac{\text{Net Profit}}{\text{Net Sales}}$

This ratio indicates the % of net profit that is earned on each dollar of sales. The higher the net profit margin the better the ratio is considered to be. Low profit margins can be an indication of a highly competitive industry structure. Low profit margins indicate that the firm should increase its sales, decrease its costs, or both. Profit margin ratios should be based on the net income from continuing operations in order to accurately reflect the firms probable profitability into the foreseeable future.

Resources

Asset Turnover $\frac{\text{Net Sales}}{\text{Total Assets}}$

This ratio measures the effectiveness of the firm's use of assets to generate sales revenue. This ratio can vary over time for a given firm. Firms in the start-up stage tend to have low asset turnover ratios, while mature companies tend to have a more stable asset turnover. Generally, a high asset turnover ratio indicates that the assets are being effectively employed; however, a high asset turnover does not explicitly take into account that the firm might be using old assets, which have been fully depreciated. A firm using newly purchased assets will show a lower turnover ratio because of the higher depreciation costs even though the new machinery is highly efficient. Firms will try to keep their long-term asset turnover ratios close to the industry norm.

Inventory Turnover $\frac{\text{Cost of Goods Sold}}{\text{Closing Inventory}}$

The inventory turnover ratio indicates the number of times that an inventory is sold and replaced over a given time period. This ratio can be used to assess the quality of an inventory. Inventory turnover ratios vary widely by industry and obvious deviations from the industry standard may indicate problems. Too much inventory can indicate improper purchasing, inadequate marketing, or an undesirable product. On the other hand, too little inventory can cause problems with product availability and can therefore hurt sales.

Receivable Turnover $\frac{\text{Credit Sales}}{\text{Closing Accounts Receivable}}$

The receivable turnover ratio measures the effectiveness of a firm's credit and collection policies. A high receivable turnover rate can indicate an effective credit and collection policy or alternatively it can indicate that a business operates on a cash basis. A low turnover rate indicates that the firm should pay more attention to collecting its accounts receivable. Accounts Receivable can amount to interest free loans to customers. The firm should analyze its accounts receivable in terms of its stated credit policy.

Debt

Total Debt to Equity $\dfrac{\text{Total Debt}}{\text{Book Value of Common Equity}}$

This debt ratio measures a firm's leverage, and is therefore an estimate of its financial risk. A high-level of debt can be a warning sign of possible problems in the future and indicates high financial risk. A high-level of debt implies high fixed interest costs, which reduces the firm's financial flexibility and its ability to pay dividends to the common shareholders. A low level of debt can indicate that management is not optimizing the firm's capital structure and is therefore not maximizing total shareholder wealth. Utility firms, which are typically highly leveraged, should not carry total debt that exceeds 1.5 times its common equity. Industrial concerns, on other hand, should not incur debt that exceeds 0.5 times its equity base.

Total Debt to Assets $\dfrac{\text{Total Debt}}{\text{Total Assets}}$

This ratio measures the level of support that is provided to the firm by its creditors. The reciprocal of this ratio is called the asset coverage ratio. The asset coverage ratio shows the amount of assets backing the companies debt and is a safety measure from a bondholder's perspective. This ratio should be calculated using total tangible assets in order to determine a conservative estimate of the firms ability to re-pay a bondholder.

Times Interest Earned $\dfrac{\text{Income from Operations}}{\text{Annual Interest Expense}}$

The times interest earned, or the interest coverage ratio, measures the margin safety for a corporation's bondholders. This ratio measures the firm's ability to pay its annual fixed interest charges from its ongoing business operations. There are no set rules determining an acceptable number of times earnings should cover interest. A bondholder should investigate the long-term trend of this ratio since it is a better indication of the firms continuing ability through good times and bad times to meet its interest obligations. As a rule of thumb, the more volatile a company's earnings, the higher the times interest earned ratio should be.

Liquidity

Current $\dfrac{\text{Current Assets}}{\text{Current Liabilities}}$

The current ratio measures the business's ability to meet its current obligations (due within the next 12 months) with its current assets. This ratio should be similar to the industry average. For many businesses, an acceptable level of coverage is on the order of 2:1. If the ratio is too low it can indicate possible solvency problems. Excessive investment in current assets, on the other hand, can indicate an ineffective use of the firm's short-term resources. A high current ratio can indicate uncollected accounts receivable, too much inventory, or it can indicate that management is stockpiling cash.

Acid-Test (Quick) $\dfrac{\text{Cash + Cash Equivalents + Accounts Receivable}}{\text{Current Liabilities}}$

The acid test or quick ratio is used to determine the business's ability to pay its current liabilities using only the most highly liquid of its current assets. This ratio is a more stringent measure of a firm's liquidity since it ignores the value of the firm's inventory. A ratio of 1:1 is considered desirable, but no single standard exists.

Working Capital

Current Assets – Current Liabilities

The working capital or net current assets are used to finance the business's cash conversion cycle i.e., the time required to convert raw materials into finished goods, to sell the finished goods, and to collect the accounts receivable. The amount of working capital required by a firm varies by industry, season, and stage of the business cycle.

Value

Dividend Payout $\dfrac{\text{Total Dividends (Common + Preferred)}}{\text{Net Income}}$

The payout ratio indicates the % of net earnings that the corporation pays out in the form of dividends to the equity owners. Growth company's usually have low or zero payout ratios. The Board of Directors of a corporation tends to prefer to maintain a steady payout ratio rather than allowing the payout ratio to fluctuate with corporations earnings. The Board of Directors of a blue-chip company does not increase dividends without considering the informational content of the dividend. Generally, when a blue-chip company increases its dividend, this signals that the Board believes that the future prospects for the business are expected to be good. The retention ratio (RR) is the % of earnings that are retained in order to finance the future operations of the business. The RR is calculated as (1-payout ratio).

$$\text{P/E Multiple} \quad \frac{\text{Current Market price of Common Share}}{\text{Earnings per Common Share (latest 12 months)}}$$

The P/E multiple or P/E ratio is calculated only for common shares. This ratio calculates the trailing P/E ratio, since it is based on the previous 12 months earnings. The P/E multiple should be used to evaluate companies which are in the same industry, in order for the results of a comparison to be meaningful. The P/E multiple varies widely from industry to industry. In simplistic terms, the P/E multiple indicates the price that investors are willing to pay today for each dollar of a corporation's earnings. The P/E multiple is one of the most widely used financial indicators or tools employed by investors.

Book Value per Common

$$\frac{\text{Total Shareholders Equity} - \text{Preferred Equity}}{\text{average number of common shares outstanding}}$$

The book value per common share is an indication of the margin of safety for common shareholders. This ratio indicates the dollar amount that would be available to be distributed to a common shareholder in the case of dissolution of the company. A more conservative estimate of the margin of safety would calculate the tangible net worth/per common share. Academic research has shown that the ratio which calculates price/book value is a good predictor of future investment results, and that stocks selling at low price/book value tend to outperform stocks selling at high price/book value multiples.

Earnings per Common Share

$$\frac{\text{Net Income (before extraordinary items)} - \text{Preferred Dividends}}{\text{average number of common shares outstanding}}$$

Earnings per common share or EPS is one of the most common financial ratios employed by investors and is frequently reported in the financial press. High net earnings per common share can indicate that management has the ability to pay dividends to the common shareholders. Conversely, low or negative EPS generally indicates that no dividends should be expected.

Market Capitalization

Current market Price of Common Share × current number of common shares outstanding

The market capitalization or market cap calculation computes the current fair market value (FMV) of the corporations common shares outstanding. Studies have shown that small cap stocks tend to outperform large cap stocks.

The purpose of financial analysis is threefold:

- to determine the growth potential of the firm,
- to determine the level of risk within the firm, and
- to determine the financial flexibility of the firm

The limitations of ratio analysis

- Large multinational conglomerates with many different business segments can be difficult to analyze. The difficulty is compounded by the investor's inability to identify comparable competitors against which to measure the conglomerate.
- Qualitative factors such as: economic and political considerations, management ability, marketing ability, and the human resources of the firm are not measured in the traditional financial statements.
- Corporate management can manipulate the financial statements by making accounting choices which are available to them and still remain within the acceptable standards required by the generally accepted accounting principles (GAAP) in order to put the best face on information contained within the financial statements.
- There is always a time delay between the end of an accounting reporting period and the actual publication of the firm's quarterly or annual financial statements. The delay can be several months.
- Management choices regarding the reporting of financial activities will vary from company to company, making comparisons difficult for an investor. For example, 2 identical corporations in the same industry may choose different depreciation rates for their equipment, or they may choose different accounting techniques for reporting inventory.
- Ratios do not necessarily disclose the quality of their components. For example, a high current ratio might mean that a company has high accounts receivable or inventories and not cash.

- Financial statements are based on historic costs and therefore may be misleading during periods of inflation.

Interpreting financial ratios

- The long-term trend of the ratios can be as important as the absolute value of the ratio itself.
- General economic conditions affect the ratios; therefore, the investor should study the ratios with respect to the stage of the business cycle.
- Ratios should be compared to industry standards or norms.
- Ratios should be compared to management's stated goals for the firm.
- Experience helps an investor to evaluate the meaning of the information contained within the financial statements.

CHAPTER 7

Estate Planning

To many individuals estate planning simply means the passing along of assets to heirs. In a larger context, however, estate planning can be thought of as every investment decision made by an investor in order to save tax dollars and to add to capital. This capital subsequently becomes the object of preservation through prudent planning. It is recommended that one involve their financial advisor, accountant, and lawyer in the estate planning process in order to ensure that all issues and circumstances are addressed and dealt with.

Estate planning and financial planning have much common:

- both are based on the attainment of objectives,
- both provide for changes in circumstances,
- both are often concerned with the minimization of income taxes, and
- both are subject to regular review and updates.

Objectives of estate planning

(1) **The identification of heirs is a major objective of most estate plans.**

This process includes not only choosing who will benefit under the will, but who will benefit during the lifetime of the individual. For example, an individual may decide to help their children to pay for their education, purchase a business, or make some other major personal purchase. Many people are prepared to split income with one or more dependents while they are still alive. Conversely, charities often benefit because individuals who have no heirs make gifts to them. A major estate planning decision, which is often difficult, is the identification of specific individuals or organizations that will be left particular assets.

(2) **Minimizing income taxes.**

The minimization of income taxes can be viewed from 2 perspectives:

- while alive, or
- at death.

While an individual is alive there are a variety of techniques which will either defer tax or shift income so that annual income taxes will be lower. Tax deferral means that income taxes must be paid at some stage and arrangements must be made so that funds will be available to pay the taxes when they are due.

At the time of death, the minimization of income taxes may come about by leaving specified assets to certain groups of taxpayers. The risk with this strategy is that it may be contrary to the individual's real wishes. Income tax may be deferred by using spousal rollover's of RRSPs or RRIFs. Otherwise, RRSPs and RRIFs are deemed to have been received upon death and must be included in the final tax return. An individual may have up to 4 separate Canadian income tax returns filed on their behalf after their death and these tax returns must be filed within 6 months of the date of death. Additionally, there may be more tax returns required if the individual had property or residency in another country.

(3) **Minimizing costs.**

Some estate plans and estate planning techniques can be virtually cost free and are very easy to administer while, at the other extreme, some plans can be very expensive to implement and to operate. For example, owning property in joint tenancy will ensure that the surviving tenant will automatically take ownership of the property upon the death of the first tenant. Although there may be other reasons that a joint tenancy might be inappropriate, this method is easy to implement. The design and implementation of a formal trust, on the other hand, can be relatively more expensive to implement and the ongoing income tax requirements will necessitate additional administration costs.

(4) **Retirement savings vehicles.**

Particular care should be given to insurance planning specifically with respect to the individual's and the survivor's rights under various government pension plans, registered pension plans, registered retirement savings plans (RRSPs), and registered retirement income funds (RRIFs).

(5) **Liquidity.**

One of the unique features of the *Income Tax Act* is its reference to what is known as a deemed realization or disposition at death. At death, there will very often be demands upon cash in an individual's estate to pay taxes, to repay debts, pay for funeral expenses, or to make cash legacies. Many individuals are asset rich and cash poor, and cash demands are an unpleasant reality.

If income taxes are minimized by using tax-free rollover's and there is little or no deemed realization, for example when everything rolls to the spouse, all that has been accomplished is the deferral of income tax until the spouse's death.

(6) **Spouses.**

Generally speaking, the wills of both spouses should be reviewed together to ensure that they operate in tandem to achieve the overall estate planning objectives.

The basic tools of estate planning

1) The Will

Financial advisors recommend that the details of a Will be discussed with family members, in advance, to prevent or to reduce future arguments and discontent. Without a Will, the identification of heirs cannot take place and provincial law determines how to divide the estate. When an individual dies without a Will, they are said to have died intestate. This may result in an apportionment that is not the individual's preference and in distributions that make poor tax and business sense.

A Will is used to:

- appoint an executor and/or possible alternative executor(s) for the estate
- nominate guardian's for minor children or other dependents
- instruct on the distribution of personal effects
- make specific bequests
- give the executor the power to administer the estate
- establish testamentary trusts, and
- guide the executor on funeral arrangements.

The executor's duties generally are to:

- locate the last Will and interpret it
- arrange the funeral
- prepare an inventory of assets and liabilities
- apply for and obtain the letters of probate, in all provinces except Quebec
- guide the estate through the probate process
- safeguard the assets of the estate
- settle all claims, debts, and expenses of the estate
- prepare and file tax returns
- obtain a clearance certificate from Revenue Canada
- keep account of assets, revenues, and expenses
- distribute assets to the beneficiaries, and
- ensure that the deceased's wishes are being met through the entire estate settlement process.

In short, the executor must ensure that all terms of the Will are met and that the estate is properly settled.

Basic clauses typically found in a Will include:

- **Identification and revocation.** In this clause the testator identifies himself and revokes all previously drawn wills.
- **Executor appointment.** This clause identifies the executor or co-executor and may waive the requirement for the appointed executor to post a bond. It is in this clause that the compensation for the executor is outlined.
- **Payments of debt.** This clause lists the sources that are to be used for the retirement of outstanding debt as well as the funeral expense and any administration costs to the estate.
- **Payment of taxes.** This clause provides for the payment of income taxes and the sources that are to be used for the payment of these income taxes.
- **Specific bequests.** This clause is used to distribute specific property to named beneficiaries.
- **Residue of the estate.** This clause provides for the disposition of the balance of the estate after specific bequests have been distributed.
- **Trusts.** This clause provides for the establishment of testamentary trusts.
- **Powers clause.** This clause grants powers to the executor so that the executor can manage the estate. Specific powers may include the ability of the executor to borrow money on behalf of the estate, invest or reinvest assets, sell property on behalf of the estate without having to apply to the probate court for the required permission. A mutual fund clause allows the executor to delegate the investment responsibility to a professional money manager; this power is required since the executor and trustees of the estate cannot delegate their responsibilities.
- **Appoint guardians.** This clause names the guardians who will care for the testator's minor or dependent children.
- **Attestation.** This clause appears at the end of the Will and acknowledges that the testator knew that he was drawing up a Will with which to distribute his estate.
- **Signatures.** The Will is signed by the testator as well as the independent witnesses to the signature.

2) Insurance

Insurance is important in an estate plan for 2 major reasons. It provides liquid funds when they are needed at the time of death. Secondly, insurance policy death benefits are not taxable. However, there are different tax consequences that flow from the manner in which policies are held, who pays the premiums, and the type of policy.

3) Gifting

Certain types of gifts may be made without tax consequences or in circumstances under which tax may be deferred indefinitely. Other gifts may result in immediate tax consequences under which the *Income Tax Act*'s income attribution rules or the deemed capital gains rules apply. It is recommended that a professional advisor be contacted before a gift is bestowed to ensure that the funds flow without triggering unforeseen income taxes.

4) Power of attorney (POA)

A power of attorney is essential for any individual who is concerned about losing control of their affairs and who wishes to minimize the expense and inconvenience of the courts supervision.

This document is important when an individual wishes to see a financial, retirement, or estate plan carried out due to reasons including illness, poor mobility, or vacations. POAs can even be used in the unfortunate event of incapacity.

There are 2 basic types of POAs; one provides authority for financial decisions and the other authorizes parties to make decisions about another's personal care.

5) Trusts

Essentially, trusts assign future control of financial assets. A trust, which is established while an individual is alive, is called an inter-vivos trust. A trust, which is established in a Will, is known as a testamentary trust.

There are three parties to a trust:

- the settlor is the party that establishes the trust,
- the trustee is the party that takes title to and administers the trust property, and
- the beneficiary who may receive capital and or income from the trust.

The establishment and monitoring of formal trusts can be a complicated and time consuming activity and it is therefore recommended that appropriate professionals such as lawyers and accountants be consulted as part of this process. This will ensure that an individual's legal and tax circumstances are adequately considered and appropriately dealt with.

Basic estate planning techniques

1) Designate beneficiaries

Assets designated to specific beneficiaries (named individuals rather than the estate) on life insurance policies, registered retirement savings plans (RRSPs), registered retirement income funds (RRIFs), annuities, and registered pension plans (RPPs) are paid or transferred directly to the beneficiary from the plan, thereby bypassing probate.

2) Income and capital shifting

Income splitting is an established technique designed to shift funds that would otherwise be taxable, to another party for three basic reasons:

- lowering of current income tax,
- maximizing deductions and credits, or
- to provide independent funding and the ability to prove the source of funds for income tax reporting purposes.

The income attribution rules prevent the shifting of income to certain individuals who are in a lower tax bracket. In addition, the income attribution rules usually operate where there is a transfer of property for the benefit of a spouse or a non-arms length minor, and occasionally where the transaction is with another non-arms length adult. Generally speaking, the income attribution rules attribute income taxes back to the transferor, or the donor, and the result is to disallow income splitting. However, specific exceptions should be reviewed with the individual's tax advisor before each income transfer to ensure that it is handled in the most appropriate fashion.

Capital splitting is a technique, such as an estate freeze, to build up an estate for beneficiaries. It is a long-term arrangement under which substantial assets will be built up in the name of the beneficiaries. The major benefit of capital splitting arises on death since the assets owned by the beneficiaries of the split will not have any deemed realization for income tax purposes, when the individual dies.

3) Tax deferral

The basic reason that tax deferral is an attractive option in estate planning can be summed up by saying that a dollar of tax paid this year is more expensive than a dollar of tax paid in the future. In other words, the time value of money must be considered. An example of a tax-deferral mechanism is a spousal rollover at the time of death.

Glossary

Abrogate. To cancel, annul, or abolish.

Addendum. An addition to a document that is usually placed at the end of the document.

Adjudication. The process by which a judgment is determined.

Advocate. An individual who represents another party in court. A lawyer or attorney at law .

Agent. An individual who represents another party and is authorized to act on their behalf.

Attest. To certify, swear to, or corroborate.

Attorney. An agent. The individual appointed to handle the affairs of another in a power of attorney. This individual need not be a lawyer.

Attorney at law. A lawyer.

Beneficiary. An individual, or party, who will gain from another.

Bequest. A legacy. Gift by Will usually in the form of money or personal property.

Capacity. Competent. Having the qualifications to exercise legal power and decision-making.

Codicil. An amendment or addition which is used to modify, rather than redraft, a Will.

Consanguinity. Blood relationship descended from a common ancestry. A consideration in the settlement of an intestate estate.

Contingent. To depend upon something which is to occur in the future and is therefore uncertain.

Convey. To transfer the ownership of, or the title to, another party.

Curtsey. The right by which a widower may inherit his wife's property after her death.

Declaring. An individual who makes a formal assertion, affirmation, or declaration.

Dower. The right that a widow is entitled to a share in her dead husband's property.

Enduring power of attorney. A power of attorney which lasts beyond an individual's mental incapacity.

Escheat. The right of the Crown to inherit and possess the property of someone who dies intestate and leaves no heirs.

Estate. An estate is composed of everything that a person owns or has an interest in including land, buildings, money, securities, and other possessions.

Executor. A male named by the maker of a Will to carry out the terms of the will.

Executrix. A female executor.

Fiduciary. A party who has the duty to act in the best interest of another. The duty arises because the fiduciary has a special position of trust and confidentiality.

Grantor. The party who creates a power of attorney.

Hereditaments. Anything that can be inherited including money, securities, or other property.

Holograph. A Will or legal document that is entirely written in long hand by the maker or grantor.

Incapacitated. The inability to perform ones duties or functions caused by physical or mental impairment.

Indefeasible. A right that cannot be taken away or revoked.

In loco parentis. In the place of a parent.

Inter-vivos trust. A trust set up during the lifetime of the individual who is creating the trust.

Intestate. The state of drying without having made a Will.

Irrevocable. Not capable of being canceled, terminated, or annulled.

Issue. An individual's descendants such as children and grandchildren.

Joint tenancy. An ownership of property by 2 or more persons.

Last Will and testament. The Will that is valid and in force at the time of death.

Legacy. Gift or bequest granted in a Will.

Legitimate. That which is recognized to be legal.

Letters of administration. Documents issued by the probate court authorizing a party to administer the estate of an individual who died intestate.

Letters testamentary or letters probate. Documents issued by the probate court authorizing the executor to administer the estate and to fulfill the terms of the Will.

Life interest. An interest in property for ones entire lifetime. Life interest does not constitute ownership.

Lineal descent. Direct line of descent that is legally important when someone dies intestate. For example, grandfather, son, grandson.

Lis pendens. Pending litigation or lawsuit.

Living Will. Statement by an individual outlining their wishes concerning exceptional efforts to maintain life.

Minor. The age under which a person is considered at law, to be legally competent. A person who is too young to make a legal contract.

Mortis causa. In contemplation of death.

Non compos mentis. Mentally incompetent. Mental incompetence includes those who are mentally defective from birth, those who have become senile, and those of unsound mind due to the use of drugs or alcohol.

Parens patriae. The right of the government to serve as guardian's for those who cannot look after themselves. For example, children and the mentally ill.

Pendente lite. An event that takes place while a lawsuit is in progress.

Per capita. By the individual or by head. Used to divide something into equal shares.

Per stirpes. Through the roots. By representation. Used to denote the share that a descendant has in a deceased person's estate.

Personal property or chattel property. Anything other than real estate that an individual can own.

Personal representative. The administrator or executor of an estate.

Power of attorney. A legal document appointing another party to act on behalf of an individual. It gives authority to the agent to carry out specific acts. The power of attorney ceases on the death of the principal or on the principal's becoming mentally incompetent.

Preferential share. The provincially specified share of an intestate's estate that is paid to a surviving spouse before any other beneficiary.

Prenuptial or premarital agreement. An agreement between a man and a woman that is reached before their marriage. It proposes to provide for the division of property in case of separation, or divorce.

Pretermitted heir. A child who has been omitted from a parent's Will.

Principal. The main person as opposed to an agent.

Probate. The legal process of validating a Will.

Pro rata. Proportionately. By percentage.

Proxy. A person authorized to act for another.

Reciprocal wills. Wills which are executed by 2 people each naming the other as beneficiary. The wills are usually identical.

Registrar. A civil servant responsible for maintaining public records.

Remainder. The portion of an estate that is to be distributed after other portions have been disposed of.

Remainderman. Someone who holds an interest in an estate in the future.

Residuary clause. The clause in a Will that disposes of the rest of the estate after settling all debts, and after all specific bequests have been made.

Residue. That which is left after all debts and legacies of the estate have been taken care of.

Revocation of the Will. The annulment of an existing Will. Revocation is usually followed by the making of a new Will.

Rights and things. Amounts, which had been earned but not yet, paid at the time of death.

§. Used in legal documents to state the place in which the document is executed.

Settlor. The individual who establishes a trust, by transferring property to the trust .

Surrogate court or probate court. Court which presides over the execution of wills and estates.

Tenancy in common. Possession of property by 2 or more people. Each party holds an undivided interest in the entire property.

Testamentary trust. A trust which is established in the Will.

Testate. One who dies with a Will.

Testator. A male who has written a Will.

Testatrix. A female who has written a Will.

Trust. The handing of property to one party, that is to be held for the benefit of another party.

Trust deed or indenture. A legal document that states the specific terms and conditions of a trust.

Trustee. A party who holds title to property for the benefit of another. A trustee is a fiduciary who acts in accordance with the terms of the trust deed.

Will. A legal document written in contemplation of eventual death that expresses the wishes of the individual who creates the Will. The Will typically deals with the disposition of property after death.

Questions

An individual has been asked to be executor of an estate. What factors should be considered before accepting the appointment?

The executor should be expected to survive the testator.

The executor must be willing and able to handle the affairs of the estate.

A corporate trustee should be considered if the estate is large or complex.

The executor is not bound to accept the appointment.

The executor must be of legal age and bondable.

Do not name a committee as executor, since decisions require all executors to agree.

It is possible to encounter a situation wherein there is a Will but no executor. This case is referred to, as administration with Will annexed.

2) Are handwritten Wills acceptable?

The Will that is entirely in the testator's handwriting and is not witnessed but is signed by the testator is known as a holographic Will. The Holograph Will is valid in some Canadian provinces but not all. A Will that is purchased from a bookstore or which is available from a CD-ROM is not considered to be a holographic Will and therefore these types of Wills must be properly witnessed.

3) What is probate?

Probate is the process whereby the court verifies that the Will is the most current available. The probate process also confirms the appointment of the executor. The document provided by the court after the completion of the process is called letters probate. The letters probate are necessary in order for the executor to complete the transactions that are required to eventually distribute the estate. Probate is not required in the province of Quebec.

4) What does intestate mean?

Intestate means that an individual died with no Will. In such cases, application must be made to the court for letters of administration. The letters of administration appoint an individual to act on behalf of the deceased, and carry the same duties as an executor. Each of the provincial governments in effect determines how, in the event of intestacy, the estate is to be distributed. A preferential share of the estate is paid, in all provinces, to the surviving spouse.

Not only does intestacy prevent an individual from deciding to whom assets are to be distributed, but it can also result in an extensive waiting period for beneficiaries and additional fees may be levied against the estate.

5) How can individuals prevent their estate going to probate?

Only assets that form part of the estate are subject to probate. There are a variety of methods of distributing assets to beneficiaries. An individual can:

- employ a bequest in the Will,
- employ a testamentary trust created in the Will,
- employ an inter-vivos trust,
- gift the assets while alive, or
- employ non-probatable assets.

Non-probatable assets would include assets that go directly to a named beneficiary such as life insurance proceeds or RRSPs and are therefore not considered part of the estate. Other assets may be held in joint tenancy with the right of survivorship, and these assets are passed outside of the Will.

6) When should an individual review their Will?

It is recommended that individuals review their Will on a periodicbasis.The Will should be rewritten whenever there is a major change to:

- the income tax status of the testator or a change in tax law,
- the marital status of the testator or any of the beneficiaries,
- the financial status of the testator,
- the province of domicile,
- the family situation of the testator such as a birth or death of a beneficiary,
- the named executor; such as the executors death.

Will checklist

- When was the Will last reviewed?
- Does the Will reflect the individuals current situation and wishes?
- Where will the funds needed to pay funeral costs and other debts come from?
- Are any charities to be benefited?
- Has a co-executor been named?
- Are there any conflicts of interest between the executor and the beneficiaries?
- Is the executor competent to deal with the estate?
- Are the appropriate powers clauses included in the Will?
- Are guardian's named for minor children?
- How does the Will deal with mentally or physically handicapped beneficiaries?
- Has the testator considered the effect of disinheriting a family member?

CHAPTER 8

Retirement Lifestyles Choices and Snowbirding

With the aging of the baby boom generation, Canada is on the verge of a dramatic increase in the number of people reaching retirement age. The first of the baby boomers are now over age 50. Moreover, within the next several decades, an unprecedented number of

Canadians will reach the "normal" retirement age of 65. Many of these individuals are already opting for early retirement. The majority of retirees choose to spend the rest of their lives in Canada, often moving out of large urban areas to smaller communities; while others opt for semi-retirement, working on a contract basis or part-time basis.

Some retirees choose to live in another country, either permanently or for part of each year. Family or cultural ties are sometimes incentives to retire abroad. Since Canadians come from all parts of the world, few nations are not potential destinations for retirement. Some of the countries that are Canada's major sources of immigrants are also the main retirement destinations, for example the USA, the United Kingdom, France, Germany, Mexico, and the Caribbean.

Severing Canadian Residency

A retiree cannot terminate their Canadian citizenship or residency simply by living in another country and becoming a legal resident of another country does not establish non-residence in Canada for income tax purposes. A retiree must demonstrate the intention to leave the country permanently. Revenue Canada determines non-resident status on a case-by-case basis, so a retiree should consult a professional advisor about the necessary steps required. Retaining Canadian residency does not necessarily put a retiree at a disadvantage. Depending on the particular circumstances, their actual tax liability could be lower than the non-resident withholding taxes imposed on Canadian pensions and investment income.

Some financial planning considerations that must be reviewed prior to permanently relocating outside of Canada are:

1. Has the retiree allowed for Canadian withholding taxes on their pension income?
2. Will the retiree be subject to double taxation in their country of destination?
3. Has the retiree arranged to file the required tax returns in Canada?
4. Has the retiree made allowances for additional communication expenses, travel costs, and import duties?
5. Has the retiree arranged for continued health care?

In general, absence from Canada for 2 years or longer is considered evidence of non-residence provided that a retiree terminates other links, such as:

- residences;
- bank accounts;
- credit cards;
- driver's licenses;
- health-plan memberships; and
- club or professional memberships.

If a retiree returns to Canada within 2 years, they will probably be taxed on the income earned while gone. A regular pattern of visits to Canada can be regarded as evidence of continued residency, especially if the retiree has family connections within Canada. If a retiree retains ownership of their Canadian home, it should be leased on a non-revocable basis; if a retiree has ongoing access to it, it may still be regarded as their residence.

Non-Resident Tax Returns

Once a retiree has become a non-resident of Canada, as defined by Revenue Canada, they are no longer required to file Canadian income-tax returns. It may, however, be in their interest to do so especially if the retiree has income that is subject to Canadian withholding tax. Withholding taxes are considered final if the retiree does not file a return, but individuals may be entitled to a refund if they file a return and their taxable income is low enough.

Canadian Departure Taxes

Taxpayers who emigrate from Canada are generally deemed to have disposed of their assets at fair market value (FMV) on the date that they leave. A deemed disposition is triggered by the declaration that the retiree has left Canada. This declaration is made on the final income-tax return, filed by April 30 of the year following their departure. Capital gains taxes, if any, are assessed at that time. Assets affected by this provision include shares in Canadian corporations, but not real estate. Those with assets valued at more than $25,000 must file a special return.

Receiving Canadian Public Pensions Abroad

Canada Pension Plan/Quebec Pension Plan (CPP/QPP) and Old Age Security (OAS) benefits can be paid to a retiree when the retiree is living outside of Canada, subject to certain conditions.

A retiree must satisfy Canada's minimum residence requirements for foreign receipt of CPP/QPP. If a retiree has lived or worked in a country with which Canada has concluded a reciprocal social security agreement, then they may qualify for social security benefits from both countries.

Canada's OAS system is intended to guarantee a minimum income to retirees, and it is subject to an income test. A retiree can receive OAS benefits outside Canada, but they must file an annual return reporting their worldwide income.

Canadian Non-Resident Withholding Taxes

Canada imposes a withholding tax on "passive" income from Canadian sources, paid to non-residents including annuity payments and pension plans. Since January 1, 1996, this withholding tax has also applied to CPP/QPP and OAS benefits. The amount of the withholding tax varies depending on the type of income, but it is 25% for pension payments. This tax may be reduced by any tax treaties between Canada and other countries.

Seasonal Retirement Abroad

Many Canadians, for whom the principal motivation for retiring abroad is climate, elect to maintain their Canadian residency and spend several months of each year in a warmer place. The southern United States is a very popular destination for these so-called "snowbirds" because it offers the advantages of geographical proximity, moderate climate, and cultural affinity. Florida and Arizona, in particular, have substantial winter populations of Canadians, as do a number of other "sun belt" states. Bermuda and the Bahamas offer the advantage of proximity for Canadians who can afford the higher cost of living in those countries. Those seeking a lower cost of living often choose Mexico, Costa Rica or other places in Latin America and the Caribbean. Destinations in the Southern Hemisphere, such as Australia, New Zealand, and Chile, while farther away, offer "snowbirds" the possibility of an almost endless summer.

Taxation Issues

The tax situation of Canadians living abroad is complicated, to some extent, by the fact that each country bases its income-tax system on different principles. Canada and the United States both tax residents on their worldwide income, and both countries tax non-residents on some types of domestic income. Many other countries however, tax only income from local sources, often because they lack the resources to assess worldwide income.

A few countries may not tax income at all, relying instead on consumption taxes and import duties. Fortunately, the situation is simplified if a retiree moves to one of the 60 countries with which Canada has a tax treaty. These tax treaties often eliminate double taxation for those who would otherwise have to pay tax on the same income in both countries. Generally, tax treaties determine how much each country can tax income such as salaries, wages, pensions, and investment income.

If a retiree moves to a country that does not have a tax treaty with Canada, they may be subject to double taxation. A retiree should carefully research the tax laws of their intended country of destination. If a retiree will be taxed on their Canadian-source income, it is important to determine if the withholding taxes that a retiree pays in Canada can be offset against their tax liability in their country of destination.

Estate Tax

Canada does not levy an estate tax, but many other countries, including the United States do. In the United States, this tax can reach 55% for large estates. If a retiree is going to become a resident of a country with an estate tax and they have substantial assets, the individual should consult a tax advisor in the country of destination. A retiree may need to have a new Will prepared or may have to make other arrangements.

The concept of Canadian residency is a taxation issue, not an immigration matter. A person is considered a factual resident of Canada if he/she "sojourns" in Canada for 183 days a year or more. Once an individual has established a home and has been employed in Canada, they cannot lose this residency status simply by leaving the country. A retiree must permanently and overtly sever their Canadian connections and declare their departure on their final income-tax return. "Snowbirds", therefore, do not have to worry about accidentally forfeiting their Canadian residency, regardless of their immigration status.

People who spend part of the year in another country but maintain their residence in Canada must pay Canadian income taxes as if they had never left. Nonetheless, taxation issues arise if the other country imposes its own taxes. If a retiree were to spend their winters in a country, which has a tax treaty with Canada, such as the United States or Mexico, the retiree is protected from double taxation, although they may have to file a tax return in both countries. If "snowbirds" are spending part of each year in a non-treaty country, they should do extensive research to find out what their tax situation is. The critical question is whether, as a retiree, their Canadian-source pensions and investment income will be taxed. Some countries impose taxes on income from the rental of a home during the off-season.

United States Tax Returns

The U.S. tax situation is worthy of special mention because parts of the United States are so popular as destinations for Canadian "snowbirds". Under certain circumstances, Canadian residents who spend part of the year in the United States may have to file U.S. tax returns. People who spend more than 30 days in the United States in a calendar year, and do not have the right of permanent residence ("green card"), are considered aliens.

An alien may be classified as resident or non-resident. In general, non-resident aliens are required to pay tax only on certain U.S. source income. Resident aliens are liable for tax on their worldwide income. A retiree can apply for an exemption from the U.S. substantial presence test by demonstrating that they maintain a more substantial connection to Canada. If a retiree is a permanent resident of Canada and has family and economic ties at home, they should be able to qualify.

Provided that a retiree qualifies, they may remain in the United States for up to 182 days each year without becoming a resident alien. If a retiree becomes a resident alien, they must file a U.S. tax return; if a retiree is a non-resident alien, they must file a tax return only if they have income from certain U.S. sources.

The most common U.S. income source for "snowbirds" is the off-season rental of their southern homes. If a retiree has this type of income, it is considered not to be connected with their presence in the United States and it is taxed at a flat 30% of the gross return. If a retiree disposes of U.S. real estate, it may be subject to capital gains tax. Any Canadian required to file a U.S. tax return must first apply for an IRS individual taxpayer identification number. However, a retiree may be eligible for relief from U.S. taxes under the Canada/United States tax treaty, since they will also have to declare all rental income and pay appropriate taxes in Canada.

Health-Care Issues

Health care is a serious issue for Canadian expatriates because few countries have systems that are as comprehensive or as inexpensive for the user as Canada's. Some developed countries have comprehensive health-care plans that will cover a retiree, after a waiting period, if they immigrate. Nevertheless, the countries that are the major destinations for Canadian retirees generally do not offer comparable programs.

Canadian provincial health-care programs provide limited coverage during temporary periods of absence from Canada. Typically, the coverage extends for three months. The level of benefits, however, may be inadequate to cover costs in some locations, especially the United States. The reason for this is that the benefits paid for out-of-country treatment are comparable to the fees paid by the provincial plans to health-care providers in Canada.

In some circumstances, a foreign hospital may charge many times as much as the provincial program will allow. It is therefore essential that a retiree arrange for private health-care insurance when living abroad. Provincial health-care programs terminate eligibility after periods of prolonged absence from Canada, typically six months. In most cases, a retiree must be physically present in their Canadian province of residence for 183 days of each calendar year in order to maintain their health-care coverage. The rationale for this is that, when "snowbirds" are out of the country, they are not paying provincial sales tax or the Goods and Services Tax, both of which help to pay for medical care.

If a retiree loses the provincial health-care coverage, there is a waiting period to requalify after returning to Canada. In most provinces, this qualifying period is three months. Supplementary private insurance sold in Canada generally will not cover a retiree during this period, because such policies are usually issued on the condition that a retiree maintain eligibility under provincial plans.

Canadian health care is mainly a provincial matter, and each province's health-care plan has its own residency requirements. A typical requirement is that a retiree is physically present in the province for at least six months a year. These requirements are not related to residency for tax purposes. A retiree can lose the entitlement to provincial health care and still be liable for both federal and provincial income taxes. If a retiree loses the provincial health-care coverage, they may have to wait three months in order to requalify for coverage after their return.

In some provinces, a retiree can avoid the requalification period by waiving their right to coverage while out of the country. This way, they will be covered immediately upon their return, although they were out of the country for more than six months. Before leaving Canada, a retiree should check with their provincial health-care authorities to make sure that they fully understand how their health-care coverage will be affected.

Private health care in the United States presents particular problems because the Health Management Organization (HMO) system that covers the majority of Americans is generally restricted to US residents with a social security number. Even then, unrestricted coverage usually ceases at age 65, when the Medicare system begins its coverage.

Private Health-Care Insurance

There are 2 types of private health-care insurance.

- Replacement insurance provides coverage for those who are ineligible for provincial plans.
- Supplementary insurance provides supplementary benefits for people who are covered by a Canadian provincial health-care plan.

Replacement Insurance

If a retiree will be living outside Canada for long enough to lose their provincial health-care coverage, they will need full replacement coverage and not just supplementary benefits. A retiree may elect to waive this temporary out-of-country coverage if their provincial plan allows it, since a retiree will need replacement coverage from the date of departure anyway. Full replacement insurance is less readily available than supplementary insurance, but there are a number of companies that provide insurance specifically designed for expatriates.

An Internet search will produce the names of several alternative health insurance providers. This search should be undertaken to ensure that individuals understand all of their options.

A retiree should arrange for replacement insurance before leaving Canada, but retirees should be aware that they may not be able to obtain appropriate coverage from a Canadian company since Canadian insurance companies are not allowed to duplicate the benefits which are provided by the provincial health plans. Most of these replacement health insurance policies reserve the right to repatriate the retiree to a country for which they hold a passport in case of serious illness or injury, and the insurer will not normally pay for treatment in Canada. This is another reason for waiving their out-of-country coverage when a retiree leaves. All of these types of health insurance policies place some limitations on pre-existing medical conditions and have age restrictions. It is possible, however, to obtain coverage from an international provider with no forced repatriation provisions that will cover a retiree up to age 75, with limited coverage for pre-existing medical conditions. The premiums for such a policy are in the neighborhood of $15,000 per year for each covered person at the higher end of the age range.

Supplementary Insurance

Even if a retiree plans to return to Canada soon enough to avoid losing their provincial health-care coverage, it is still advisable to have private health-care insurance, mainly to cover the extra cost of medical services received abroad. Supplementary insurance offers benefits for people covered by a Canadian provincial health-care plan. This type of insurance is relatively inexpensive since it covers only unexpected short-term health problems.

A retiree is expected to return to Canada for treatment of pre-existing medical conditions or long-term health problems. Most of these policies include coverage for emergency evacuation to Canada and, in many cases, evacuation is mandatory for serious problems. A retiree can claim the cost of foreign medical expenses, **including insurance premiums**, as an income-tax deduction. A retiree should obtain supplementary insurance before leaving Canada.

Health-care insurance checklist:

- Will the insurance plan pay foreign hospital and related medical costs directly?
- Is medical evacuation to Canada covered?
- Are pre-existing medical conditions covered?
- Will the insurer provide the cash deposits required by some hospitals?
- Are costs associated with a death abroad, including the return of remains to Canada, covered?
- Is service available on a round-the-clock basis?
- Does the insurance package cover flight cancellations for medical reasons?
- What will a retiree do if they have an accident or become ill?
- Are they prepared for emergency repatriation?
- Has the retiree checked the provisions of their provincial health-care plan?

Real Estate Issues

For many Canadians, owning their own retirement home is part of their dream for an ideal retirement. This is also a practical issue since good rental accommodation is usually expensive in the most popular destinations; especially as furnished homes are often the norm for expatriates. While it is prudent to rent for a time before deciding on a particular location, eventually purchasing a condominium or a house is an option that many retirees will consider.

Canadian residents who own property abroad are required to report their foreign assets to Revenue Canada. This is a recent provision, designed to ensure that residents declare capital gains and interest on foreign assets on their Canadian income-tax returns. The regulations were originally introduced in 1996, but implementation was delayed, and the first reporting deadline was April 30,1999. All Canadian taxpayers with foreign property valued at more than $100,000 are required to report their holdings, and there are substantial penalties for non-compliance.

Property Ownership

Purchasing property in some countries can be risky because of the difficulty in obtaining clear title. Careful research and professional legal advice are essential to prevent a retiree from falling victim to unscrupulous operators. In some countries, a retiree can buy title insurance.

The right of foreigners to buy certain property is restricted in some countries. In Mexico, for example, foreigners require special permits to buy land. They cannot own land within a 100-kilometer band along the borders or a 50-kilometer zone along the coasts. In addition, they cannot own mineral or water rights. They may, however, set up trusts to hold restricted property for them.

It is difficult for foreigners who are not locally employed to obtain conventional mortgage financing in most countries. If a retiree still has Canadian residency status, their Canadian bank may extend a personal loan based on their Canadian assets and their credit rating.

Condominiums

In principle, condominiums offer many advantages to retirees. External maintenance is handled on a shared basis, and it is relatively safe to leave units unoccupied for extended periods. On the other hand, condominiums can entail serious risks in countries with little experience in administering the relevant laws.

A retiree cannot assume that condominium by-laws drafted by property developers will actually be enforceable. Indeed, some restrictions, such as those prohibiting occupancy by children, may contravene local laws. Condominiums in developing countries tend to be occupied by foreigners from many parts of the world, and these people may have very different ideas about the use of common property. Many condominiums have rental units available, and leasing one before buying is the best way to check out not only the property, but the community as well.

Immigration and Citizenship Issues

Retirees who live in another country for less than six months each year can simply visit that country as tourists. Most countries welcome Canadian visitors who come for recreational purposes, and a valid passport is usually the only requirement. The United States does not require Canadian visitors to have a visa.

Mexico is also open to seasonal Canadian visitors. A Mexican tourist card is good for 180 days and can be obtained at any port of entry. Many countries have limitations that are more stringent on the length of time that visitors may stay. For example, the Bahamas permits visitors to stay up to a total of eight months a year, but each entry is limited to four months or less. Costa Rica allows visitors to stay for up to 90 days.

In some cases, a retiree can lengthen their stay by applying for an extension from within the country, but this is not always possible. Mexico, for example, will extend tourist visas beyond 180 days only for emergency medical reasons. Many Canadians are reluctant to settle in a country where they have the right of entry only as tourists, especially if they are planning to purchase a home. Some people deal with this issue by applying for residency status, although they fully intend to maintain their Canadian residency.

In Canada, residency is a matter of fact, not law, whereas in many other countries a resident is a person who has a resident visa or residency permit but does not actually reside in that country for a significant time. Taking out legal residency in another country does not interfere with one's Canadian residency. Holding resident status in the country where the retiree maintains their winter home eliminates limitations on the length of their stays there. It also gives a retiree reasonable assurance that they will be allowed entry, usually without a return ticket. In some cases, a retiree may also be allowed annual duty-free exemptions.

Voting

Canadian citizens can, under certain conditions, vote in Canadian elections when they are temporarily living abroad. The general requirement is that their last stay in Canada was within the previous 5 years, and that their intention is to resume their Canadian residency. In order to vote, a retiree must first register at a Canadian diplomatic or consular mission, and they will be required to provide proof of Canadian citizenship. A retiree will then be provided with a voting kit for an election, by-election, or referendum. The onus is on the retiree, as the voter, to return the ballot in time for it to be delivered in Canada on the day of the election.

Extended vacation planning

Items which should be arranged before leaving on an extended vacation

Cash management

1. Ensure that travel and health insurance have been purchased.
2. Ensure that all bills and expenses are either pre-paid or redirected to someone who will make payments.
3. Bank accounts should contain enough funds to pay bills while out of town and to provide sufficient funds upon return.
4. It is recommended that travelers carry at least one credit card that can be used in case of emergency. The credit limit on the card should be sufficient to bear a reasonable number of expenses.
5. Purchase travelers checks in appropriate denominations and currencies.
6. Ensure that sufficient cash is carried, enough to cover several days of expenses.
7. Ensure that income-tax installments, GST payments, and income-tax return (T1) preparation is taken care of.
8. If traveling with others, consider splitting travelers checks and credit cards between parties for safety in the event of theft or loss.
9. Purchase a travel wallet to be worn under garments to store important papers and cash.
10. Powers of attorney (POAs) should be prepared to ensure that financial affairs are taken care of while absent.

Leaving home

1. Make arrangements for mail delivery or pick up and forwarding.
2. Discontinue newspaper delivery to the vacant home.
3. Ensure that a friend or family member has a set of keys to the home and is instructed to check the premises on a regular basis.
4. Some travelers arrange for a lamp to be connected to a timer, so that a light is activated each evening in the home for a specified period of time.
5. Advise trusted neighbors that you will be out-of-town.
6. Arrange for snow removal from sidewalks and the driveway while the home is vacant.
7. Store valuables and important papers in a safety deposit box.
8. Some travelers prefer to unplug TVs, computers, and other appliances during their absence.
9. Ensure that the homeowners property insurance policy allows for extended vacation without jeopardizing coverage.
10. Ensure that the home is protected against pipes freezing and any other potential mechanical problems.

Miscellaneous items

1. Ensure that passports and visas are in hand several weeks before departure. Experienced travelers know that passports should not expire within six months of the anticipated return date.
2. If leaving a vehicle at home, it should be started occasionally to avoid battery problems.
3. Plan wardrobe and incidental requirements ahead of time so that purchases can be made over a reasonable period of time.
4. If driving, ensure that the vehicle has a full maintenance check up including installation of snow tires, if required, before leaving home. Map a route in advance and check for road repairs and closures. An auto club will often offer services that map the shortest or most scenic routes to the final destination.
5. If flying to the final destination, ensure that all flights are prearranged, paid for, and departing on time according to the ticket details.

6. Be prepared to pay any airport or port taxes that may be charged.
7. Ensure that family members and loved ones have a telephone number and address at the final destination. Often, the credit card companies provide emergency message services.
8. Purchase sufficient quantities of prescription drugs.
9. Ensure that all required inoculations and vaccinations are current.
10. Ensure that Wills are current.

Questions

1) Why would an individual purchase out of country medical insurance if they are just traveling on vacation for 2 weeks?

Poor health or accidents can occur at anytime, even when traveling out of the country for short periods of time. Generally, health care is expensive outside of Canada particularly when an individual is hospitalized for an emergency or if surgery is required.

2) What is a snowbird?

A snowbird is an individual who travels from the snowbelt to a warmer climate, usually to enjoy an extended vacation. Canadian snowbirds tend to flock to popular sunshine destinations such as Florida, Arizona, or California.

CHAPTER 9

Strategies

The following strategies should be considered when planning for early retirement.

Cash Management

Does the individual have a monthly budget?

- A budget will help to identify where cash is being spent on a monthly basis. It will also help to identify any funds that the individual has which are in excess of committed expenditures, and which can therefore be saved on a regular basis. It will also aid the individual in identifying their debt service ratio, and their ability to take on additional debt or to retire outstanding debt.

Can the individual reduce current consumption in order to increase savings?

- The use of a monthly budget will help to identify where the income is spent. One great advantage of this exercise is the identification of non-essential current consumption. It often results that an individual, when faced with their current spending habits, recognizes that certain items of current consumption may be forgone, without affecting their current lifestyle, in order to increase their savings.

Does the employer provide any payroll savings programs?

- Payroll savings programs are an easy method to accumulate capital. The great secret behind payroll savings is the fact that the individual is paying themselves first. Additionally, if an individual contributes to a registered retirement savings plan (RRSP) by payroll deduction, it may be possible to apply to have their payroll taxes reduced and therefore benefiting immediately from the tax savings rather than having to wait until their tax return has been filed. Individuals who purchase Canada savings bonds (CSBs) by payroll deduction, are able to claim the interest as a deductible tax expense since the first year's interest is added to the principal amount and used to compute the required payment which is deducted each pay period.

Can any assets be sold or repositioned in order to achieve better investment returns?

- Nonproductive investment assets can be repositioned into income producing investments if additional income is required. Poorly performing investments should be repositioned in order to maximize investment returns. Moreover, non essential luxury "toys" might be sold in order to free additional funds for investment since these types of goods often require the individual to spend additional amounts of cash for example, a boat must be moored and insured.

What should an investor focus on when analyzing their personal financial statements?

- On the net worth statement, the investor should focus on maximizing their investable assets and reducing outstanding debt. Frequently individuals will focus their attention and efforts towards maximizing total net worth. This is inefficient because total net worth can be increased if one counts or includes personal use assets such as furnishings, clothing, and vehicles. Unfortunately at retirement the individual is unlikely to liquidate these sorts of assets in order to generate retirement income. The important focus during an individual's accumulation phase should be the maximization of investable or financial assets which, at retirement, will be used to generate the income that is necessary for a comfortable lifestyle. On the cash flow statement, or in the operating budget, individuals should focus on discretionary spending and determine whether or not this discretionary spending is appropriate.

Tax Planning

Is it possible to defer compensation in order to reduce income taxes?

- An individual who can control their income for example, a business owner, may be able to defer part of their compensation into another taxation year in order to reduce their current income taxes. Investment income, such as capital gains, is triggered when the investment is disposed of. Since the individual can control this action the individual can therefore control and defer any potential income taxes until such time as the individual chooses.

Are there any income splitting opportunities available?

- The income attribution rules generally act to reduce income-splitting opportunities however; it may be possible to structure an individual's affairs in order to maximize the income splitting opportunities. It may be possible to employ a spouse or one's children; funds invested on behalf of minor children into capital gain producing assets are not subject to the income attribution rules.

Insurance and Risk Management

Can insurance deductibles be increased?

- Careful review of existing insurance coverage may point to opportunities for additional savings. Insurance deductibles reflect that part of a claim which the insured is willing to self-fund, and the higher the deductible the lower the premium. Be sure to check homeowners policies, automobile policies, and the elimination period on private disability coverage.

Can more efficient life insurance coverage be purchased?

- A careful review of policies and a current needs analysis will indicate whether term insurance or permanent life insurance coverage is required. An individual should purchase the type and amount of life-insurance coverage that is appropriate. Term insurance is most efficient when large amounts of coverage are required for short or known time frames. On the other hand, permanent insurance coverage is most efficient when funding enduring insurance needs such as a lasting and non-temporary requirement for cash with which to pay capital gains taxes, in order to preserve an estate.

Retirement Accumulation

Is the individual eligible to participate in employer-sponsored retirement programs?

- If eligible an employee should participate in all savings programs offered by an employer since these programs have the advantage of payroll deduction. Retirement programs generally must be contributed to by the employer, which translates to mean that another source in addition to the employee is paying to fund the employee's retirement. An individual should carefully study employee benefit documentation in order to ensure that they fully comprehend the value of the benefits provided. Many individuals, who do not fully understand the benefit programs, are easily misled and are in fact making lifelong decisions without understanding all of the implications and ramifications involved.

Has the individual considered selling their home and downsizing to a smaller home?

- Many individuals as they age no longer wish to or are unable to perform all of the work that is necessary in order to maintain a family home. These individuals often opt to downsize their homes and move into smaller condominium style housing where the maintenance is performed by others. It is not unusual to encounter seniors who no longer are able to climb stairs and are therefore more comfortable in a smaller home that is on a single level.

Has the individual considered a reverse mortgage?

- The reverse mortgage is a method of increasing current income without having to vacate the family home.

Has the individual investigated the use of the pension maximization (backed annuity) strategy to increase retirement income?

- This strategy is feasible if the annuitant has a permanent, and fully paid up, life insurance policy. The pension maximization strategy involves both spouses waiving the joint survivor option on a pension plan and the annuitant instead purchases a life only annuity. The rationale is that both spouses benefit while the annuitant is alive since the life only annuity will pay higher current income than the joint survivor option, everything else being equal. The life insurance policy proceeds are used to purchase additional retirement income for the surviving spouse after the death of the annuitant. Warning! The life insurance policy on the annuitant's life must be permanent coverage since term insurance can be out-lived. The permanent life insurance coverage should be paid up so that premiums are no longer payable after the annuitant's retirement. This strategy ensures that the couple has the maximum amount of retirement income possible.

Are RRSP contributions being maximized?

- As soon as is possible an individual should make maximum contributions to an RRSP each year. Unused contribution room means that the individual it is not maximizing the tax deferred advantage offered by the RRSP. Furthermore, the individual will be subject to enticement, to borrow in order to catch up and the interest incurred on this type of borrowing is not tax deductible.

Are spousal RRSPs being utilized?

- Spousal RRSPs offer the advantage of income splitting opportunities.

Investment Planning

Does the investor have realistic expectations with respect to future investment returns?

- Numerous studies recently completed in the United States indicate that many novice investors have unrealistic expectations regarding investment performance. One of the simplest methods of ensuring realistic expectations on behalf of an investor is to read and to increase their own investment knowledge. Knowledgeable investors also tend to be less panicked when investment returns fluctuate dramatically.

Has the investor considered the effects of inflation on the performance of an investment portfolio?

- Knowledge is the best defense.

Does the individual's risk tolerance allow for investments that are more aggressive in order to achieve higher rates of return?

- Modern portfolio theory is based upon the premise that the investment return is directly related to the investment risk. Beware! An investor who takes greater risk is not guaranteed a higher return.

Has the individual investigated the tax benefits of investing in Canadian dividend producing corporations?

- Dividends paid by taxable Canadian corporations are subject to the dividend tax credit (DTC). Under the current Canadian tax law, dividends from Canadian corporations attract the least amount of income tax of any type of investment income. This is true no matter which province the investor lives in and regardless of the investor's income level. Warning! Canadian dividend producing equities held within an RRSP do not qualify for the dividend tax credit. Investors holding these types of investments within their RRSPs are therefore missing a fabulous tax advantaged incentive. Investors should carefully evaluate the structure and the holdings of their portfolios and should, where possible, hold equity investments outside of RRSPs and RRIFs and hold interest-bearing investment such as bonds and certificates within the registered plans, in order to maximize the tax deferral available from these vehicles.

Estate planning

Has the individual considered having more than one Will?

- Canadians who own property outside of Canada should consult their professional advisors in order to determine whether it would be advantageous to draft a Will which deals with the foreign property.

Is a power of attorney valid in all Canadian provinces?

- It is imperative that anyone considering drafting a power of attorney seek legal advice since the provincial laws which govern the creation and use of the power of attorney vary from province to province.

Has the individual considered a testamentary letter?

- A testamentary letter is an explanation, in plain language, which lays out the testator's wishes with respect to his estate. The testamentary letter can be of great value to the executor, but be warned that the testamentary letter does not replace a Will.

USEFUL WEBSITES

Canadian commercial rating services

Canadian bond rating service (CBRS).
http://www.cbrs.com

Dominion bond rating service (DBRS).
http://www.dbrs.com

Tests, Ratios, Analysis and Charts Insurance Services Ltd. (TRAC).
http://www.trac.com

Credit & Debt

Canada Mortgage and Housing Corporation (CMHC).
http://www.cmhc-schl.gc.ca

Managing Your Money.
http://www.cba.ca/eng/Tools/Brochures/tools_manage.htm

Mortgage Wise.
http://www.cba.ca/eng/Tools/Brochures/tools_mortgage.htm

Credit Counselling.
http://creditdoktor.org/

Department of Justice

Laws of Canada.
http://canada.justice.gc.ca/Loireg/index_en.html

Statutes.
http://canada.justice.gc.ca/FTP/EN/Laws/index.html

Economics

Bank of Canada.
http://www.bank-banque-canada.ca/english/intro-e.htm

Board of Govenors of the Federal Reserve System.
http://www.bog.frb.fed.us/default.htm

Ed Yardeni of Deutsche Bank.
http://www.yardeni.com/

CIA Handbook of Economic Statistics.
http://www.cia.gov/cia/di/products/hies/index.html

Statistics Canada.
http://www.statcan.ca/start.html

The White House Briefing Room.
http://www.whitehouse.gov/WH/html/briefroom.html

Estate Planning

BC Law Society.
http://www.acjnet.org/dialalaw/bc.html

BC Legal Information Centre.
http://wwlia.org/cabchome.htm

Estate Planning for Farm Families.
http://www.agr.gov.sk.ca/

Law Society of Upper Canada.
http://www.lsuc.on.ca/public_en.shtml

Public Trustee of BC.
http://www.trustee.bc.ca/

Snowbirding.
http://www.crossborder.com/ctf959USEP.html

Wills in Canada.
http://wwlia.org/ca-wills.htm

Finance

Finance Sites for Students.
http://web.utk.edu/%7Ejwachowi/wacho_world.html#INDEX

Interactive Financial Math tutorials.
http://www-ec.njit.edu/~mathis/interactive/index.html

Teach Me Finance.
http://www.teachmefinance.com/

Terry Gordon's Finance Links (BCIT).
http://home.istar.ca/~jtgordon/bcit/links.htm

The Interest in Your Life.
http://www.cba.ca/eng/Tools/Brochures/tools_interest.htm

Valuation, Investment and Finance.
http://www.stern.nyu.edu/~xadamodar/

Insurance

Benefits Canada.
http://www.benefitscanada.com/

Canadian Life and Health Insurance Association (CLHIA).
http://www.clhia.ca

CompCorp.
http://www.compcorp.ca

Employment Insurance(EI).
http://hrdc-drhc.gc.ca/ei/common/home.shtml

Insurance Bureau of Canada.
http://www.ibc.ca/english/intro.htm

Medical Information Bureau(MIB).
http://www.mib.com/sitemap.html

Medicare Canada.
http://www.hc-sc.gc.ca/medicare/home.htm

Investment

Bonds in Canada.
http://www.bondcan.com/

Canada Deposit Insurance Corporation (CDIC).
http://www.cdic.ca

Canada Mortgage and Housing Corporation (CMHC).
http://www.cmhc-schl.gc.ca

Canadian Depository for Securities (CDS).
http://www.cds.ca

Canadian Investor Protection Fund (CIPF).
http://www.cipf.ca

Canadian Payment Associations (CPA).
http://www.cdnpay.ca

Canadian Securities Administrators (CSA).
http://www.osc.gov.on.ca

Canadian Shareowner's Association.
http://www.shareowner.ca/

Credit Union Deposit Insurance Corporations (CUDIC).
http://www.caseybyte.com/cucc

Harvard Business School.
http://www.hbs.edu/applegate/bizinfo3/

Investment Research via the Internet.
http://www.ibbotson.com/Research/iafp96.htm

Investment Theory.
http://viking.som.yale.edu/will/finman540/classnotes/summary.html

Investors Learning Centre.
http://www.investorlearning.ca/ilc/plsql/pub_admin.ILC_main_page

Office of the Superintendent of Financial Institutions (OSFI).
http://www.osfi-bsif.gc.ca

Ontario Securities Commission (OSC).
http://www.osc.gov.on.ca

System for Electronic Document Analysis and Retrieval (SEDAR).
http://www.sedar.com

Retirement & Pensions

Canada Pension Plan(CPP).
http://www.hrdc-drhc.gc.ca/isp/common/cpptoc_e.shtml

Old Age Security(OAS).
http://hrdc-drhc.gc.ca/isp/oas/oasind_e.shtml

Pension Benefit Standards of BC.
http://www.labour.gov.bc.ca/psb/welcome.htm

Pension Sector (FSCO).
http://www.ontarioinsurance.com/Pensions

Retire Web.
http://www.retireweb.com/

Stock Exchanges — Canadian

Alberta stock exchange (ASE).
http://www.ase.ca

Montreal stock exchange (ME).
http://www.me.org

Toronto stock exchange (TSE).
http://www.tse.com

Vancouver stock exchange (VSE).
http://www.vse.ca

Winnipeg stock exchange (WSE).
http://www.wse.ca

Stock Exchanges — International

Bourse de Paris.
http://www.bourse-de-paris.fr

Frankfurt (DAX).
http://www.exchange.de

Italian stock exchange.
http://www.borsaitalia.it

London Metal Exchange (LME).
http://www.lme.co.u

London Stock Exchange (LSE).
http://www.londonstockex.co.uk

Stock Exchange of Hong Kong (SEHK).
http://www.sehk.com.hk

Tokyo stock exchange.
http://www.tse.or.jp

Stock Exchanges — U.S.

Securities and Exchange Commission (SEC).
http://www.sec.gov

Electronic Data Gathering Analysis, and Retrieval (EDGAR).
http://www.sec.gov/edgarhp.htm

New York Stock Exchange (NYSE).
http://www.nyse.com

Chicago Board Of Trade (CBOT).
http://www.cbot.com

American Stock Exchange (AMEX).
http://www.amex.com

NASDAQ.
http://www.nasdaq.com

Miscellaneous

Canadian Society of Actuaries.
http://www.actuaries.ca/mape.htm

Canadian Tax Foundation.
http://www.ctf.ca/

CCH Canadian.
http://www.ca.cch.com

Consumer Affairs.
http://strategis.ic.gc.ca/sc_consu/consaffairs/engdoc/oca.html

Dept. of Finance.
http://www.fin.gc.ca/fin-eng.html

Health Canada Online.
http://www.hc-sc.gc.ca/english/

Larry J. Stubbs. larrystubbs@yahoo.com

Ontario Consumer Protection.
http://www.ccr.gov.on.ca/mccr/welcome.htm

Revenue Canada.
http://www.rc.gc.ca/menu/EmenuZZZ.html

TOPICAL INDEX